IT'S OKAY NOT TO BE OKAY IF...

WILLIAM E. BERG

LUTHERAN
COLPORTAGE
SERVICE, INC.

ABOUT THE COVER

Hopefully, the stained glass window will bring light on the title and message of this book.

This window, together with the Good Shepherd and Ascension windows, is located in the beautiful sanctuary of the Augustana Lutheran Church in Minneapolis, Minnesota. The author served as Senior Pastor there for fifteen years. Among many cherished memories are the "stained glass window tours" he conducted for hundreds of persons during those years.

In the sanctuary we saw the Son of God on His cross of torture and shame. We saw the price He paid to rescue us and our fallen human race. We saw the Good Shepherd, whose arms protect us. We saw the ascending Christ going back to His Father's house. There He is preparing a place for us in Paradise.

Many persons in need of food, counseling and financial help came to the church, and we tried to fulfill their physical needs. Recognizing their deeper spiritual needs, we invited many to the sanctuary to see and hear the story of the windows. The most exciting part of the tour was when the Lord stepped out of the windows and met many who remained at the altar to pray.

In his sixty-five years of ordained ministry, the author has tried to keep the crucified and risen Saviour sharply in focus in his preaching and teaching. For it is at the cross that we find the transforming power of self-giving love. At the cross we find the divine incentive for proclaiming the "greatest story ever told". This is the cross that "towers o'er the wrecks of time".

In the light of the cross we see the shallowness of the doctrine of cheap grace. There we find exposed and discredited the notion of "coercive grace". This is a contradiction in terms. Its adherents believe that persons will be saved in their unbelief and in their rejection of Jesus as Saviour and Lord. Coerced goodness is not goodness, and false assurance is the dangerous gift of false prophets who miss the heart of the gospel.

At the cross the author learns who he is, a died-for and forgiven sinner on his way to Paradise Regained. But he knows that he must do more than look at the cross and handle the Holy Book. His hands must be free for unfinished tasks, free to reflect the self-giving love of Jesus and free to be servants in His work of healing and reconciliation in our world.

"So they strengthened their hands for the good work."
NEHEMIAH 2:28

*The cover reveals the hands
of our Saviour nailed to a cross.
May our hands be ready for
the unfinished tasks He has for us.*

TABLE OF CONTENTS

DEDICATION

In my book, *Show Me the Way to Go Home*, I have written in some detail of my thirty-year journey with E. Stanley Jones.

For readers not acquainted with him, the following information will make this dedication more meaningful to them.

Dr. Jones served as a missionary to India for over sixty years. During these years he also conducted evangelism missions across the United States, in Europe, South America, Africa, Japan (ten evangelistic tours there) and other places. He was indeed a world missionary and evangelist. And more. He was a pioneer in the struggles for racial justice and integration. Sixty years ago, his Christian Ashrams, south or north, were always inter-racial and inter-denominational. He worked tirelessly for peace and freedom in the world. For many years he worked with Mahatma Gandhi for the liberation of India. In the fall of 1941, he worked with President Franklin Roosevelt and his staff in a desperate effort to avert World War II. He wanted to get a message through to the Emperor of Japan who was worshipped as god. He believed that the emperor alone could control the powerful military force. He called it an adventure in failure. He was nominated for the Nobel Peace Prize.

He founded the International Christian Ashram movement. From Gandhi and the Hindu Ashram, he saw the value of a "time exposure to God" through silence, meditation and reflection. The name "Ashram" comes from the Sanskrit. Its root is "a", from, and "shram", hard work, meaning a retreat or time apart from the pressures and distractions of everyday life for physical and spiritual renewal. In the Hindu Ashrams, Gandhi was the center around which all teaching revolved. In bringing the Ashram to the USA in 1940, Stanley Jones said, "No man is wise enough or good enough to be the center of a religious movement—only divine shoulders can bear that responsibility." Jesus Christ is the center of the Christian Ashram. In the early morning quiet time, we sit in corporate silence in His presence. Then we share with the group what He has given us. In the Bible study sessions, we meet Jesus, our teacher. In the prayer and share groups, we do not spend time in dialogue or unfocused conversation. We are there for prayer and praise, together bringing our burdens, blessings, deep needs and answered prayers to Him who is able to supply every need. In the 24 hour prayer vigil, each person is alone in the presence of the Lord of Glory. In the healing services, we meet the healer and are anointed, not into what we want, but into His perfect plan for body, mind and spirit. In the church-at-work hours, we tell of specific and practical ministries that our Lord has used in local parishes to fulfill our high calling there. The high point in the schedule of worship services comes in the Holy Communion service. There, we receive the visible word, His body and blood for the forgiveness of our sins, for life and salvation.

I started reading Dr. Jones' books in 1935 while still in the seminary. I heard his message for the first time in person in 1943. His magnificent obsession with the Kingdom of God, with the Lordship of Jesus Christ and with the Word made Flesh, reflected for me the eternal Word of our God and made a deep impression on my ministries. His 28 books have provided invaluable resource material for me and for many.

In 1972, I served as Chairman of the first International Christian Ashram held in Jerusalem. Dr. Jones, confined in a wheelchair following a severe paralytic stroke six months earlier, was present. He gave a memorable keynote message, long to be remembered by the 325 members in attendance.

I also served as Chairman of the International Christian Ashram in India in 1974 and in Japan in 1978. In these Ashrams, the spiritual impact of Dr. Jones' ministry was impressive indeed. Other high points for me were to serve on his Ashram teams in Sweden, Washington, DC and Minneapolis, Minnesota.

Following his death, I recall a scene in a Baltimore cemetery in 1973. In a processional from Dr. Jones' home church, we walked to the cemetery carrying part of the ashes of his earthly body. (Some were taken to Sat Tal in India.) We sang his favorite hymns as we marched. We shared great passages of life and hope from the scriptures. I thought, as I was taking my turn in carrying the precious urn, "Brother Stanley, you helped carry me so many times in my pilgrimage. Our Lord used you to lift and carry countless multitudes closer to Him. Rest in peace until the Resurrection morning and the beginning of your new career of service in the Father's House."

In this dedication message, I thank our Lord for countless Christian Ashram partners across the whole world, friends who have blessed and lifted me. I close by quoting the Christian Ashram prayer that is used before each meal:

"We thank Thee, Lord, for daily bread
For all thy blessings 'round us spread.
We bless Thee for thy love and care,
For guidance in the hour of prayer.
For Ashram comrades eager, true,
For love's unfinished work to do.
In all we think and do and say,
Thy Kingdom come in us today." Amen

FOR LOVE'S UNFINISHED WORK TO DO. I pray that the writing of this book may be part of my unfinished work.

Just as the earthly ministry of Stanley Jones was finished in 1973, your work and mine will come to an end in our Lord's time. May we remember to praise Him for LOVE'S UNFIN-ISHED WORK TO DO in this world. May we look forward with great expectation to the continuing ministries He will have for us in Paradise Regained.

There we shall join with the angels and all the redeemed, including loved ones gone before, in His nearer Presence in a celestial celebration of praise.

"Worthy is the Lamb who was slain,
to receive power and wealth and wisdom and might
and honor and glory and blessing!"
REVELATION 5:12

I praise my Lord for "Brother Stanley" who helped me see more clearly the Unshakeable Kingdom and the Unchanging Person.

E. STANLEY JONES
My Spiritual Mentor for thirty years

Seventy years in the ministry of the Methodist Church.

Author *Missionary* *Evangelist*
Apostle
Founder of Christian Ashrams
Ecumenical leader
Bishop-elect
Statesman
Witness for Christ
Spokesman for peace, racial brotherhood and social justice

BORN	**DIED**
January 3, 1884	January 25, 1973
Clarksville, Maryland, U.S.A.	Bareilly, U.P., India

Jesus is Lord

"Jesus is Lord—Lord of the past, Lord of the present, Lord of the future. Jesus is Lord of everything. Jesus is Lord, unqualified. What a conclusion! A conclusion which is a beginning. A testimony of faith by STANLEY JONES

PREFACE

Several years ago, I visited the Vasa Ship Museum in Stockholm, Sweden. There I heard and saw the story of the famous ship which was equipped with cannons designed to make the Swedish Navy master of the seas.

Completed in 1628, it was dedicated with great fanfare, led by King Gustav V. Just seven hours after the launching, the top-heavy ship sank. Three hundred years later, with brilliant technology, the ship was raised from the bottom of the sea and completely restored.

Upon hearing this story, a friend said to me, "Those Swedes must be very stupid to build a ship like that." I replied, "Perhaps so, and yet they were smart in raising the large ship, now seen and admired by throngs of tourists.

Applying this story to my life, I need to ask, "Am I smart or stupid to be writing another book at my age of 92?" Perhaps I can give the same answer as I gave to the tourist.

Maybe I am smart, or at least intellectually and spiritually aware, because this writing ministry, I believe, comes out of an irrevocable call of my Lord.

Now the word "stupid" is a strong word. Some of the dictionary synonyms are: "foolish, irrational, lacking a sense of intelligent perception or awareness". Hopefully, I am not in this category.

I want to assure my readers that I do not feel "smart" or wise enough or qualified enough to write a book on the **Divine IFs**. I must admit that in the writing of this book, disturbing questions have come to my mind. Will the title bring support to those who believe that they are okay just as they are, without any need of a divine Creator and Saviour? Will some readers be turned off by negative thoughts such as, "You're okay if you do this and do not do that?" I have come through this intellectual and spiritual crisis in my study of the **Divine IFs**. Let me explain.

Each morning I sing sixteen stanzas set to the tune, "This Is The Day That The Lord Has Made". I sing in the midst of inevitable impairments that I wish were not there. I praise our Lord for sixteen gifts that make it exciting and hopeful for me to begin the day. These gifts are Day, Place, World, Body, Family, Church, Nation, Person, Promise, Way, Feet, Hands, Mind, Friends, Song and Love. On several of these gifts I have to stop and meditate. One of the stopping places every morning is, "This is the mind that the Lord has made". The Bible verse that goes with this gift is Luke 24:45:

> *"Then he [Jesus] opened their minds*
> *to understand the scriptures."*

It is not enough to pray for open-mindedness. I pray for a mind opened by our Lord and His Spirit for the purpose of understanding what He is saying to us in His Word. Of course, in this fallen world we "see in a mirror darkly", and our spiritual and intellectual understanding is partial and incomplete. In writing this book, I pray daily for divine grace to write, speak, teach and read with a mind open to the scriptures. If this prayer is fulfilled, this book will be worth writing and reading.

Another incentive for writing this book is the fact that I cannot recall having read or heard of a book specifically on the **Divine IFs**. I have long believed that our Lord's **Divine IFs** are His very special gift to us. They help keep us honest, rational, positive and realistic in our Christian faith. If we omit the **Divine IFs**, we are in danger of becoming false prophets who misquote the Bible. For example, on the program of Columbia University's anniversary celebration were quoted these words of Jesus, "The Truth Shall Make You Free". A friend of mine wrote to the Dean of the University, "You are misquoting the Biblical passage in John 8:31 and 32. You left out the all important word *if*.

> *"**If** you continue in my word,*
> *you are truly my disciples,*
> *and you will know the truth,*
> *and the truth will make you free."*

We need to remember that the death sentence of Jesus was based on misquotations of false witnesses. This is a deadly sin with severe consequences, both for the one who misquotes the Bible and the one who hears it.

Someone may be asking, "Is not God's love unconditional?" Indeed it is. But I believe that the **Divine IF** magnifies Divine Love. God's love honors us with the gifts of responsibility and accountability. He treats us as persons capable of making choices.

Would you like to see the wonder and glory and majesty and might of our God and Creator? We are indeed saved by faith, but it is faith that becomes sight by the grace of God. This faith is a free gift which our Lord offers to us with His **Divine IF**.

> *"Did I not tell you that **if** you would believe*
> *you would see the glory of God."*
> JOHN 11:40

I hope that the title of this book reveals to us the fact that any person born into this fallen world is a "not okay" person. This is in accordance with the Word of our Lord in Romans 3:10-12:

> *"None is righteous, no, not one; no one understands,*
> *no one seeks for God. All have turned aside, together they*
> *have gone wrong; no one does good, not even one."*

And in Romans 3:23, we read these words:

> *". . . all have sinned and fall short of the glory of God."*

This sounds like depressing news. Are we not called to give good news? To me, in light of the title, the message of this book is good news, namely, that I am a sinner in need of being saved. We cannot talk about anything or anyone being found unless something or someone is lost. Good news! My Lord makes me, a lost and condemned creature, eligible for His Amazing Grace!

I am grateful that our Lord does not use coercion to get us into His Kingdom. He honors us as the highest in all of His creation by giving us freedom of will.

Each morning in my devotions I sing a confession of faith. It was written many years ago by Dr. Conrad Hoyer. One of the stanzas goes like this: "I believe with all my reason, I believe with all my will, I believe with all my feelings, my whole self I yield Him still." Indeed, volition and will are vital in the Christian faith.

Many years ago I heard of a marriage service held on a very warm evening. The bridegroom was perspiring. When the pastor asked this question, "John, wilt thou have Mary to be your lawful, wedded wife," John responded, "I wilt!" This answer had negative connotations. We can say with the lost son in the far country, as we read in Luke 15:18, "*I will arise and go to my father,*" or we can see our hopes and dreams wilt into despair. The **Divine IFs** can haunt us or help us. And if someone should say, "How can I possibly accept unconditional love with a **Divine IF?**" There is an answer in Philippians 2:13:

> *"For God is at work in you,*
> *both to will and to work for his good pleasure."*

I felt deeply constrained to write this book also because of the "cheap grace" that has become so popular in our day. Dietrich Bonhoeffer, in his book, *The Cost of Discipleship*, gives a much-needed reminder:

> "Cheap grace is the preaching of forgiveness without requiring repentance, baptism without Church discipline, communion without confession, absolution without contrition. Cheap grace is grace without discipleship, grace without the cross, grace without Jesus Christ, living and incarnate."

Hopefully, the thoughts I have shared thus far will give you, the readers, a clue as to the rationale for this book.

As in my other books, I have included many quotations from other writers. I have always believed that my thoughts need to be supplemented by the wisdom of others. In fact, one of the purposes of my books is to acquaint readers with great writers like E. Stanley Jones, Max Lucado, Oswald Chambers, C. S. Lewis and others. In using quotations, we are exceedingly careful to obtain credit and to seek permission from writers and publishers.

I should add that one of the brightest features of this book is the poetry by my life partner, Marta. She was a talented writer of narrative verse. Her two books, *Seen and Unseen* and *From Grey to Gold*, tell of her brilliant mind, her spiritual discernment and her heavenly thoughts given in down-to-earth terms. One of my treasured possessions is a book of eloquent comments from countless friends who tell what her poems and insights have meant to them. So I predict that you, the readers, will not only be grateful but deeply moved by Marta's inspired writing. She left for her Heavenly Home on Thanksgiving Day, 1996.

Surely the Bible passages interspersed throughout this book are indispensable in making it worth writing and reading. Hopefully, I have been led by the Holy Spirit into His fountain of truth. During the writing of this book, I have been reassured and strengthened by these promises:

> *"Thus says the Lord: 'Let not the wise man glory in his wisdom, let not the mighty man glory in his might, let not the rich man glory in his riches; but let him who glories glory in this, that he understands and knows me, that I am the Lord who practices steadfast love, justice, and righteousness in the earth; for in these things I delight,' says the Lord."*
> JEREMIAH 9:23,24

> *"I will instruct you and teach you the way you should go; I will counsel you with my eye upon you."*
> PSALM 32:8

Those **Divine IFs**! Will they be stumbling blocks or stepping stones, helping us grow towards spiritual maturity?

How can we be sure that all of us "not okay" persons can be made okay? Amazing Grace is the answer. The logo on the cover is the answer. Those two-letter words are part of the answer: *so loved, in Christ, by faith, God is* and of course the key word *if.*

The Addendum was written after the terrorist attack on our country on September 11, 2001. Hopefully, it will give a divine perspective of the tragedies and triumphs of our day.

Coming back to the opening illustration, I repeat the question, "Is it smart or stupid for me to be writing on this subject at my age?" Let me share that I get much inspiration from a good friend, Dr. Theodore E. Conrad. At the age of 96 years and confined to his wheelchair and "scooter", this theologian, scholar, college and seminary professor keeps very busy. He writes letters for Amnesty International, keeps in touch with his 20 grandchildren and 45 great grandchildren, participates in study groups and is a tower of spiritual strength wherever he goes. In September of 2001, he spoke to a church group on the theme, "Behold the Lowly Ice Cube." This was a brilliant message filled with scientific knowledge and the miracle of God's creation. It ended in a way we shall never forget, closing with the *WATERS OF BAPTISM.*

Following this message, I signed him up to speak to the same group in September, 2002. He has already announced his topic, "Behold, the Lowly Hard Boiled Egg". I am sure that when the egg cracks, it will reveal eternal truth. Of course, both of us are aware of the fact that neither of us may be on this earth in September, 2002. The other day in his room in the Augustana Health Care Center, we were listening to a recording of a Christian hymn that we seldom hear any more, "There's A Land That Is Fairer Than Day". Both of us were thinking of our beautiful life partners who are in the nearer presence of the Lord on that farther shore. And it goes without saying that we long to join them there and to see our Saviour face-to-face. However, until our time of departure comes, our Lord has continuing ministry for us.

I would like to think that this book is part of His continuing ministry for me. May it be so.

ONLY BY THE GRACE OF GOD!

WHAT DO YOU MEAN

CHAPTER ONE

BY OKAY?

Even at the age of ninety-two, I recognize that I am still "under reconstruction". I hope that I am capable of creative change and of growing toward maturity. So it is time to change the greeting that I use here, "Are you okay?" I have come to the conclusion that it is neither as helpful nor as "user-friendly" as I thought it might be. If someone would answer my question with this answer, "It depends on what you mean by okay," he or she would be doing me a big favor.

———◆———

"We are Christ's ambassadors. God is using us to speak to you: we beg you, as though Christ himself were here pleading with you, receive the love he offers you – be reconciled to God. For God took the sinless Christ and poured into him our sins. Then, in exchange, he poured God's goodness into us."
II CORINTHIANS 5:20,21 (TLB)

WHAT DO YOU MEAN BY OKAY? ⳽

In the Augustana Apartment Center where I reside, we have over five hundred residents in four connected buildings. I can walk three blocks inside to the Augustana Health Care Center where some three hundred persons are cared for. From my building at one end of the complex, I walk through the spacious dining room and through corridors lined with stores, a bank, beauty shop and offices. On these walks, I meet dozens of persons, many who are friends and some whom I do not know personally. I have been greeting friends with this question, "Are you okay?" Many respond, "I'm okay. Are you okay?" The other day a friend responded with words to this effect, "No, I am not okay. I feel awful." That was an honest answer which I appreciated. There is another answer that I would like to hear, "What do you mean by okay?" All too often we get into the lamentable practice of using words without adequate knowledge.

I recall the story of a pastor who asked the boys in a Sunday School Class, "Who broke down the walls of Jericho?" One little boy replied, "Pastor, I didn't do it." The pastor was concerned about this reply. He went to the boy's Sunday School teacher and told him of the response to his question. The Sunday School teacher said, "Pastor, that boy is one of the best behaved boys in my class. I know that he would not do such a thing." By this time, the pastor was deeply grieved. He went to the boy's parents and told them the story. The father said, "Well, I don't know whether Jimmy really did it or not, but if he did, just have somebody fix the walls and we will pay for all repairs."

We need to ask the question that we find in Job 42:3:

> *"Who is this that hides counsel without knowledge?*
> *Therefore I have uttered what I did not understand,*
> *things too wonderful for me, which I did not know."*

Words without knowledge. The following words were no doubt spoken by a man who knew some interesting theological words. I do not have the origin of these words, but they might have been spoken in a theologian's dream. He was addressing the Lord and said, "You are the eschatological manifestation of the karigma in whom we find ultimate meaning which impinges upon our interpersonal relationships." As the story goes, Jesus said, "What?"

Even at the age of ninety-two, I recognize that I am still "under reconstruction". I hope that I am capable of creative change and of growing toward maturity. So it is time to change the greeting that I use here. I have come to the conclusion that it is neither as helpful nor as "user-friendly" as I thought it might be. If someone would answer my question, "Are you okay?" with this answer, "It depends on what you mean by okay," he or she would be doing me a big favor.

I have been preaching sermons for some seventy years, hopefully messages from the Lord and His Word. I cannot recall ever being interrupted in my pulpit ministry by someone standing and saying, "Pastor, exactly what did you mean by what you just said? I do not understand what you were getting at."

Would I be upset by such an intrusion on my carefully crafted sermon? Would I be defensive? Perhaps I would be tempted to give a condescending reply, "Sir, please come to my office at the close of the service, and we will discuss your question." If I try to clarify the meaning of my words, I might only compound the confusion.

A friend told me of extending this friendly greeting to a stranger, "Have a good day." The man responded angrily, "Don't tell me what to do!" A better reply would have been, "What do you mean by a good day?" It will not help much even if we say, "I hope that you will have a good day." Someone's idea of a good day and mine may be quite different. Often when I say good night to friends in the nursing home or apartment center, I put it this way, "Have a good night," which being interpreted means, "I hope you have a 'God bless you and keep you' night."

In my apartment center, we use the checking system. Each day at 9:00 a.m. and 9:00 p.m., if I am the checker of the month, I look for the sign outside apartments on my floor. I look for the "OK" sign. If there is no "OK" sign, I will knock on the door or call by phone to see if the resident is in. If there is no response, I will call a staff person to go in and check the apartment.

I have what I call a "checking plus plan". Each evening about 10:00 p.m., following my late night walk, I stand in the two corridors of my floor for a roll call. I pray for the persons in eleven apartments. This is my nightly litany of praise, "Thank you, Lord, that you are there with Cora, Ruth, Dora, Axel, Edwin, Joan, Lucille, Victor, Ottilie, Helen, Gordon, Ethel and Dorothy." It is reassuring for me to know that their Lord and Saviour and Friend is there with them, caring for body and spirit. I also call the roll of friends in my corridors who have departed this earthly life, thanking our Lord for their memory and ministry.

I have shared these thoughts, hoping that they may be, not a digression but rather some progression toward answering the question, "What do you mean by okay?" Let us now turn to the dictionary for a definition. Here we find that the letters "O" and "K" were first used in the name of a Democratic Club. It was called the O.K. Club. The first recorded meeting was on March 24, 1840. The letters "O" and "K" are an abbreviation of Old Kinderhook which was the name of the native village of Martin Van Buren whom the O.K. Club supported for a second term as President of the United States. O.K. came to mean all right; correct; approval; endorsement. Instead of the letters O.K., the word okay came to be used.

Is this the final answer to the question, "What do you mean by okay?" I hope not. We need to go much deeper in order to adequately define what it means to be okay. In this book, we are seeking "ultimate okayness". This is a gift which only our Lord and Creator can bestow. In the Book of Life we find pictures of "okay persons".

> "Put on then, as God's chosen ones, holy and beloved, compassion, kindness, lowliness, meekness, and patience, forbearing one another and, if one has a complaint against another, forgiving each other; as the Lord has forgiven you, so you also must forgive. And above all these put on love, which binds everything together in perfect harmony. And let the peace of Christ rule in your

hearts, to which indeed you were called in the one body. And be thankful. Let the word of Christ dwell in you richly, teach and admonish one another in all wisdom, and sing psalms and hymns and spiritual songs with thankfulness in your hearts to God. And whatever you do, in word or deed, do everything in the name of the Lord Jesus, giving thanks to God the Father through him."
COLOSSIANS 3:12-17

"We are Christ's ambassadors. God is using us to speak to you: we beg you, as though Christ himself were here pleading with you, receive the love he offers you—be reconciled to God. For God took the sinless Christ and poured into him our sins. Then, in exchange, he poured God's goodness into us."
II CORINTHIANS 5:20, 21 (TLB)

The word "okay" is a universal word. My grandson, Jeff Carlson, has traveled in many countries, usually for the promotion of human rights. He gave the following information on the word "okay."

"I have heard it said that the word 'okay' is the most commonly understood word in the world, followed closely by the words 'Coca-Cola'. My own travel experience confirms this hypothesis, as I have heard the word used commonly in Japanese, French, Spanish, Norwegian and even Hindi. Accents and pronunciations change, but in all languages the meaning is the same: all right, no problem, '*okay*'!"

This word is both comforting and confusing. It is reassuring in its approval and disturbing in its vagueness. It is a unifying word describing everyone as okay. It is a devisive word in which arrogant humans divide people into those who are okay and those who are not okay.

Here is a reminder of the purpose of this book by way of a story. A pastor called the children to the front of the sanctuary for the children's sermon on a Sunday morning. He said, "Children, what is furry, has a bushy tail and climbs trees?" One little boy yelled, "Jesus!" The pastor was shocked. He said,

"Johnny, why did you say Jesus?" Johnny replied, "Well, I didn't think you called us up here to tell us about a squirrel."

I want to thank Johnny for reminding me that I am not writing this book simply to tell readers about the word **okay**. In the next five chapters, there are additional words, each with two letters. They are: **IF, SO, IN, BY** and **IS**. They are words that bring us into the presence of **God** our Father and Creator, **Jesus** our Saviour and Lord, and the **Holy Spirit** our Counselor and Guide. Here we find what it means to be really okay. So I start this journey into divine okayness with a prayer in my heart and mind. It's one of the great prayers in the Bible. It is found in Ephesians 3:14-19:

> *"For this reason I bow my knees before the Father, from whom every family in heaven and on earth is named, that according to the riches of his glory he may grant you to be strengthened with might through his Spirit in the inner man, and that Christ may dwell in your hearts through faith; that you, being rooted and grounded in love, may have power to comprehend with all the saints what is the breadth and length and height and depth, and to know the love of Christ which surpasses knowledge, that you may be filled with all the fullness of God."*

I read this story in a nursing home news letter. An employee at the airport check-in gate said, "Has anyone put anything in your baggage without your knowledge?" "If it was without my knowledge, how would I know?" answered the traveler.

The question I am asking myself as I start writing this book is, "Without knowledge, how would I know if I'm okay or if anyone else is okay?"

The answer does not lie in self-help, although this can be an important part in the healing process. It does not lie in the wisdom of psychiatrists and professional researchers of the human mind, although some of them can be of significant help. We find this reassuring answer:

> *"For it is the God who said, 'Let light shine out of darkness,' who has shone in our hearts to give the light of*

the knowledge of the glory of God in the face of Christ."
II CORINTHIANS 4:6

To be okay means more than divine knowledge. Divine knowledge leads to "okay action". To be okay means that we are called to follow the One who gave His life to save us from being "not okay" and lost. When we live in the light of the glory of God in the face of Christ, we see His face turned irrevocably toward Jerusalem where He gave His life as a ransom for us "not okay", lost sinners. The Risen Saviour turns to us in Matthew 28:19, 20:

"Go therefore and make disciples of all nations,
baptizing them in the name of the Father
and of the Son and of the Holy Spirit,
teaching them to observe all that I have commanded you;
and lo, I am with you always, to the close of the age."

Trusting in His word and in His resurrection power, we shall be free to serve Him and to help others to affirm, "I'm okay in Him!"

IF...

Many Christians wonder about the word **if**. I can hear them asking, "Is not the love of God unconditional? Do we not live by free grace? Do we not create a paradox when we bring in a condition reflected in the word **if**? There is no contradiction if we accept our Lord's unconditional love with His **Divine IF.** Think of the incredible optimism our Lord reveals, and what a high honor He bestows upon us sinners to treat us sinners——us "not okay" persons——as capable of accepting accountability and responsibility. He treats us as persons with God-given potential to respond to His love on His conditions.

"If we confess our sins, he is faithful and just, and will forgive our sins and cleanse us from all unrighteousness."
I JOHN 1:9

IT'S OKAY NOT
TO BE OKAY IF...

The word "Uffda" is a little word often carelessly used. Inasmuch as my national background is Scandinavian, I am acquainted with this word. This word is not in the dictionary, but it is an all- purpose expression covering a variety of situations. For example, when Swedish meatballs were served at a Norwegian lefsa supper, someone said, "Uffda". Someone else said, "'Uffda' is not being Norwegian."

Sometime ago I called upon an elderly friend in a nursing home. During our conversation, she said, "Uffda". I should have asked what she meant by this word. Now let me share an "Uffda" story which possibly will be more confusing than clarifying. However, I think that the lesson of the story can be related to that little word **if**. I do not know the origin of this story, and I know there are other versions.

A man purchased a horse from a friend who promptly gave him some important instructions on riding the horse. He said, "This horse will respond to two words only. If you want him to go forward, you say, 'Uffda'. If you want him to stop you say, 'Sto'." The new owner got on the horse and shouted "Uffda". The horse bounded ahead. The more he shouted "Uffda", the faster the horse galloped. He was having a great time shouting "Uffda" and enjoying the fastest ride he ever had on horseback. They went up the side of a mountain, climbing and racing upward as the shout reverberated, "Uffda". The rider looked up and remembered that at the top of the mountain there was a steep precipice. He thought it was time to stop the horse, but he forgot the word that would stop him. He and the horse approached the top of the mountain and were about to go over the steep cliff. Suddenly, he remembered the word and shouted, "Sto!" The horse stopped right at the edge of the cliff. The man looked down the steep incline, wiped his brow and said, "Uffda!" We can imagine what happened after that!

We see from this story that the word "Uffda" can be as a positive word and also as a dangerous word. Its meaning depends upon how and where it is used.

Likewise, the word **if** can be used to indicate spiritual progress or spiritual danger and destruction. For some these **ifs** can be reassuring and for others intimidating and disturbing.

We find examples of Biblical **ifs** in the First Epistle of John, chapter 1, beginning in verse 6:

> "**If** we say we have fellowship with him while we walk in darkness, we lie and do not live according to the truth."

According to this **if**, we are living a lie. Then we go to verse, 7:

> "But **if** we walk in the light, as he is in the light,
> we have fellowship with one another,
> and the blood of Jesus his Son cleanses us from all sin."

Here we have a life-giving **if**. Another example from this chapter is in verse 8:

> "**If** we say we have no sin, we deceive ourselves,
> and the truth is not in us."

Here we have the **if** of self-deceit and living in a world of delusion. We go on to verse 9:

> "**If** we confess our sins, he is faithful and just and will
> forgive our sins and cleanse us from all unrighteousness."

Here we have a reassuring **if**. How grateful we should be for these **ifs** of divine grace!

Many persons would no doubt like to get rid of those troublesome and convicting "**ifs**". Among them are advocates of divine grace without human accountability. The result of such flawed thinking is "cheap grace". A poem by Marta Berg, "Law and Love" from her book *From Grey to Gold*, can help us at this point:

> "'He broke the law.'

Oftentimes we hear these words.
But no. Not so.

God's law never breaks.
But many times man breaks himself upon the law.

God's law is written
into the very fabric of the universe.
It is sure and changeless as anything in all creation.

Sometimes we forget that disdain for His law
begets its own penalty.

We forget and, though we mean well,
we help no one
when we are so tolerant
and so loving
that we embrace the sin
as well as the sinner.

We say, 'God loves you,'
and fail to add the words,
'Go and sin no more'."

Many Christians wonder about the word **if**. I can hear them asking, "Is not the love of God unconditional? Do we not live by free grace? Do we not create a paradox when we bring in a condition reflected in the word **if**?" There is no contradiction if we accept our Lord's unconditional love with His **Divine IF**. Think of the incredible optimism our Lord reveals, and what a high honor He bestows upon us to treat us sinners—us "not okay" persons—as capable of accepting accountability and responsibility. He treats us as persons with God-given potential to respond to His love on His conditions. One of the gifts of divine grace is the gift of free will. It's the gift of choice that makes us truly human. Without this gift of free will, we become automatons, to be manipulated as robots.

All too often we seek to impose our "human **ifs**" on others. Perhaps we should call them "inhuman **ifs**". Indeed, they are destructive and demeaning. Here are some examples. A mother said to her disobedient and unruly young son, "**If** you are bad, mother can't love you." She sent him to his room. Later, she went up and found him in the bathroom, standing on a stool before the mirror. Through his tears he was singing, "Jesus loves me this I know—Jesus loves me when I'm bad."

A mother said to her misbehaving daughter, "God is very angry with you when you're bad like this." This is a good place to continue our study of the "**Divine IFs**". Without these Biblical **ifs**, our sinful, conditional **ifs** can easily give a child an inferiority complex and a feeling of never being okay unless he or she measures up. It is easy to misunderstand the meaning of divine grace. Divine grace is greater than our sins, greater than our unworthiness, greater than our failures and our straying away. Indeed, we are loved unconditionally, but divine grace is not cheap grace. It would be cheap if there was no **Divine IF** to go with it.

St. Paul writes in Romans 5:10,11:

> *"For if while we were enemies we were reconciled to
> God by the death of his Son, much more, now that we
> are reconciled, shall we be saved by his life. Not only so,
> but we also rejoice in God through our Lord Jesus Christ,
> through whom we have now received our reconciliation."*

Joy and reconciliation come to believers through the atoning death of Jesus. Without a view of the Son of God, suffering on a cross of torture and shame, we cannot possibly understand the meaning of grace and unconditional love.

We read in Matthew 7:11:

> *"If you then, who are evil, know how to give good gifts to
> your children, how much more will your Father who is in
> heaven give good things to those who ask him!"*

This is unconditional love indeed for us "not okay" persons who are willing to ask for help. Asking indicates a need. Honest asking indicates an openness to help that is offered. It means being willing to be made new on the inside. This is in accordance with the **Divine IF** in II Corinthians 5:17:

*"Therefore, **if** any one is in Christ,*
he is a brand new creation;
the old has passed away, behold, the new has come."

What does this "newness" involve? Here I quote from a sermon by Pastor Ross Foley of Faith Covenant Church in Burnsville, Minnesota. The title of this sermon is "Why Should We Be Good?"

"A little girl on the way home from church turned to her mother and said, 'Mommy, the preacher's sermon this morning confused me.' Her mother asked, 'Oh. . .why is that?' Her daughter replied, 'Well, he said that God is bigger than we are. Is that true?' 'Yes, that's true,' the mother answered. 'He also said that God lives within us. Is that true, too?' Again the mother replied, 'Yes.' 'Well,' said the girl, 'if God is bigger than us and He lives within us, wouldn't He show through?'

"The scripture was right when it said, 'Out of the mouths of babes. . .' That little girl put her finger on a very important truth. God's Spirit lives within us. His presence and power are made available to us in relation to our willingness to be obedient to His demands upon our lives. As we are obedient, His presence will show through us to others around us.

"So I say, welcome to Pentecost! It's time to open up to the mind-blowing, heart-warming, life-changing power of God. The power of God can invade the body, inflate the mind, swell the soul, lift the spirit, and make us more than we ever imagined. The Holy Spirit will make you young when you're old. He'll make you live when you die. The power and presence of the Spirit will disturb, delight, and deliver us from sin.

"When God sends forth the Spirit, chaos is changed into creation. The Red Sea opens up to a highway to freedom. A young woman says, 'Yes.' Jesus is born and life is never the same. When God sends forth the Spirit, amazing things happen. Barriers are broken. Communities are formed. Opposites are reconciled. Unity is established. Disease is cured. Addiction is broken. Cities are renewed. Races are reconciled. Hope is established. People are blessed. And church happens.

"Today the Spirit of God is present as He is every time we

come to worship. So be ready. Get ready. God is up to something. Discouraged folks, cheer up. Dishonest folks, 'fess up. Sour folks, sweeten up. Closed folks, open up. Gossipers, shut up. Conflicted folks, make up. Sleeping folks, wake up. Lukewarm folks, fire up. Dry bones, shake up. Pew potatoes, stand up. But most of all, when the Holy Spirit is present, Christ the Savior of the world, is lifted up."

All this—**if**. **If** what? **If** we believe that Jesus was lifted up on a cross, and **if** we are willing to ask, and after asking, to receive.

There are some important **ifs** in the letter of James. In this letter, chapter 1, verses 5 and 6, we read:

*"**If** any of you lacks wisdom, let him ask God, who gives to all men generously and without reproaching, and it will be given him. But let him ask in faith, with no doubting, for he who doubts is like a wave of the sea that is driven and tossed by the wind."*

In James 1:26, 27, we have this word:

*"**If** anyone thinks he is religious, and does not bridle his tongue but deceives his heart, this man's religion is vain. Religion that is pure and undefiled before God and the Father is this: to visit orphans and widows in their affliction, and to keep oneself unstained from the world."*

Also, in James 2:14-17:

*"What does it profit, my brethren, **if** a man says he has faith but has not works? Can his faith save him? **If** a brother or sister is ill-clad and in lack of daily food, and one of you says to them, 'Go in peace, be warmed and filled,' without giving them the things needed for the body, what does it profit? So faith by itself, **if** it has no works, is dead."*

I am grateful for the letter of James. It is clear to me that he does not write of human works and merit as the way of salvation.

Faith and works are inseparable. Indeed, ***faith works!*** He writes in James 1:25:

> *"But he who looks into the perfect law, the law of liberty,*
> *and perseveres, being no hearer that forgets but a doer*
> *that acts, he shall be blessed in his doing."*

In these "**ifs**" from the book of James, divine grace is magnified as our Creator and Lord honors us by giving us grace to respond—grace to ask, grace to be a doer of the word and not a hearer only, grace to obey.

Another invitation to respond is found in John 7:37:

> *"On the last day of the feast, the great day,*
> *Jesus stood up and proclaimed,*
> *'If any one thirst, let him come to me and drink.'"*

In the 1950's, while serving as Director of Evangelism in my National Lutheran Church body, the Augustana Lutheran Church, I prepared an annual study guide for use in the observance of the week of prayer. The title of one of the manuals was, *If My People Pray,* based on II Chronicles 7:14:

> *"**If** my people who are called by my name*
> *humble themselves, and pray and seek my face,*
> *and turn from their wicked ways,*
> *then I will hear from heaven,*
> *and will forgive their sin and heal their land."*

Here are the six chapter headings: "**If** My People Pray—They Will Turn, **If** My People Pray—They Will Seek My Face, **If** My People Pray—They Will Be Aware, **If** My People Pray—Their Hearts Will Burn, **If** My People Pray—Their Feet Will Go, and **If** My People Pray—Their Lives Will Glow."

If my people pray, they will be aware. In the Garden of Gethsemane, Simon Peter fell asleep at the place of prayer. He soon crashed at the place of apostasy and profane denial of His Lord. Out of touch with the suffering Saviour, he was out of touch with Life.

Surely, prayerlessness is one of the most dangerous and devastating sins. But take courage, all you who have fallen asleep at the place of prayer, and who have neglected the Saviour's admonition to "Watch and pray." Remember this, that Jesus did not come back and scold Peter and the other two sleeping disciples. He did not berate or lash out at them. Rather He said, "Rise, let us be going." Ahead was the cross of torture and shame—ahead were suffering and death. But ahead were also the resurrection, the great commission to Simon Peter, Pentecost, and a new day of opportunity when the once-sleeping disciple prayed and preached and witnessed with such power and passion that thousands came into the Kingdom. **Arise! He gives us another chance!**

To pray and to be aware mean also to care. Miriam Teichner, whom we could not reach for permission, has written these lines under the title, "Awareness":

> "God—let me be aware.
> Let me not stumble blindly down the ways,
> Just getting somehow safely through the days,
> Not even groping for another hand,
> Not even wondering why it all was planned,
> Eyes to the ground unseeking for the light,
> Soul never aching for a wild-winged flight,
> Please, keep me eager just to do my share.
> God—let me be aware.

> "God—let me be aware.
> Stab my soul fiercely with other's pain,
> Let me walk seeing horror and stain,
> Let my hands, groping, find other hands,
> Give me the heart that divines, understands,
> Give me the courage, wounded, to fight,
> Flood me with knowledge, drench me in light,
> Please, keep me eager just to do my share.
> God—let me be aware."

Jesus gives us a reassuring and life-giving **if** in Revelation 3:20:

"Behold, I stand at the door and knock;
if any one hears my voice and opens the door,
I will come in to him and eat with him, and he with me."

It's a big **if**. It is a "divine conditional **if**". We who are sinners and "not okay" persons are the only ones who can open the door to the Stranger of Galilee, the King of Glory. He comes in as our guest and we set the table for Him with precisely what He is there to receive from us: our sin, our guilt, our failures, our doubts and unbelief. Then, He becomes the host and we are His guests. At His banquet table, He provides forgiveness, absolution, acquittal, a not-guilty verdict, life and hope and peace and joy, and sufficient grace for every need and circumstance in this fallen world.

We talk about divine grace and unconditional love. Is there any greater picture than Jesus just standing at the door, waiting for us to open to Him? Hopefully, the **Divine IFs** we have presented here reflect His Amazing Grace and His love that will never let us go.

A poem by Rudyard Kipling reminds us of some human **ifs**.

"If you can talk with crowds and keep your virtue,
  Or walk with kings—nor lose the common touch,
  If neither foes nor loving friends can hurt you;
  If all men count with you, but none too much,
  If you can fill the unforgiving minute
  With sixty seconds' worth of distance run,
  Yours is the Earth and everything that's in it,
  And—which is more— you'll be a Man, my son!"

It is utterly impossible for the human mind and spirit to do what Rudyard Kipling speaks about. I believe that in our human power we will stumble over these **ifs** into failure and disillusionment. This surely magnifies our need to turn to the scriptures and to the **Divine IFs.** We turn again to I John 1:7:

*"But **if** we walk in the light, as he is in the light,*
we have fellowship with one another,
and the blood of Jesus his Son cleanses us from all sin."

On Maundy Thursday, we gather for a celebration of His Last Supper, the Holy Eucharist. Hopefully, in our spirit, we hear the singing of the hymn as they went from the Upper Room into the darkness and terrible agony in the Garden of Gethsemane. Here I do not see my Saviour kneeling at a convenient rock. Rather, I see Him writhing on the ground, face down in the dust. He was going down under the load of our sins. Indeed, we were there helping to crush the Son of God and the Lord of Glory.

Here we have an eloquent reminder of the divine cost of the Eucharistic Meal—the price He paid to reassure us "not okay", penitent guests with these words, "Take and eat, take and drink. This is my body and blood given and shed for you for the remission of your sins."

There is a song entitled, "According to Thy Gracious Word".

"Gethsemane can I forget,
    Or there Thy conflict see,
Thine agony and bloody sweat,
    And not remember Thee?

"Thy body, broken for my sake,
    My bread from heav'n shall be;
Thy testamental cup I take,
    And thus remember Thee.

"And when these failing lips grow dumb,
    And mind and memory flee,
When Thou shalt in Thy kingdom come,
    O Lord, remember me!"

Now it is time for us to ask the question, "What does this picture of Gethsemane and the cross have to do with the **Divine IF**?" **If** we accept the reality of our Lord's redemptive act on the cross, then surely we will accept the **Divine IF** in I John 1:9. As we confess our sins, we will also claim that He is faithful and just and will forgive all our sins. He will cleanse us from all unrighteousness. Jesus was faithful to the divine plan to use the cross to bring the human race back into a saving relationship with God.

He is not only faithful; He is just. There is a divine system of justice. We have not only a loving God but also a just God. Take a long look at the cross again. There we see the evil nature of sin. We also see the inflexibility of divine justice. Above all, we see "love divine, all loves excelling" and love without limits. In I John 1:7, we read that the blood of Jesus, God's Son, cleanses us from all sin. The word "sin" is not popular in our day nor in any day. Many try desperately to get rid of the word, and yes, to get rid of sin. They try to mythologize it, legalize it and institutionalize it. Some commercialize it and some demonize it. (The devil made me do it.) Others try to camouflage sin. Because it is such a harsh and unpopular word, pornography is called art, lying is called propaganda and obscenity is called freedom of speech. License comes across as liberty and lust as love. Abortion is called termination of pregnancy and prejudice is camouflaged as individual rights. But there is only one way to get rid of sin. We find it in the words of Isaiah 53:4,6:

> "Surely he has borne our griefs and carried our sorrows;
> yet we esteemed him stricken, smitten by God, and
> afflicted. . . All we like sheep have gone astray;
> we have turned every one to his own way;
> and the Lord has laid on him the iniquity of us all."

It is important to remember that we are to confess our sins, sins of the spirit and sins of the flesh. In the Christian Ashram, founded by the late Stanley Jones, we begin on the first evening with the Hour of the Open Heart. We share personal needs as we are led, although most of our needs can be taken to our Lord who has a private office. We answer the questions, "Why did you come, what do you want, what do you really need?" All of us are members in good standing of the Fellowship of Need. At the first Christian Ashram I attended in 1943, I sat in a back row thinking that it is not proper for me, a Lutheran pastor, to tell publicly of any personal need that I have. The first time I shared I told of a sophisticated, nice sounding need. It did not take me long to be convicted of the sin of "lust for vindication" and the egocentric desire to reflect a nice Christian image. There can be no healing without revealing. I found that my willingness to open my heart to others, as the Holy Spirit directed, helped me immeasurably to keep open before God. Identifying my personal needs was motivation to spend much time as a penitent at the throne of grace.

The **if** of I John 1:9 is inseparable from the **if** of verse 7, *"If we walk in the light, as he is in the light, we have fellowship with one another, and the blood of Jesus his Son cleanses us from all sin."* Walking in the light means walking with Jesus who is the Light. It means to walk in the light of His Word, to walk at the place of worship and prayer. It means to walk to the telephone to call someone in need. It means to walk to your desk to write to someone who needs a word of hope. It means to walk to someone who needs to hear your friendly greeting and to see your smile. Someone may say, "But I can't walk. I'm in a wheelchair. I'm confined to my bed." Here is good news. In Jesus, you can be a "wheelchair blessing"— a person empowered, not a person impaired!

There is another important word in verse 7. It is the word fellowship. *"If we walk in the light, as he is in the light, we have fellowship with one another."* It is a fellowship of sinners who daily are being cleansed of all sin. However, we need to remember that one of the conditions for being members in good standing of the Church, the body of Christ, and the Fellowship of the Redeemed is to come to terms with the **Divine IFs.**

Back in 1936 before blood banks were available, I was wheeled into an operating room to lie beside a woman facing surgery for cancer. The blood flowed from my body directly into her body, and she became well. Many weeks after this event, she came to the Holy Communion table where I was assisting the pastor in the distribution of the elements. For her, blood meant life physically. As she knelt at the altar and heard the words, "This is my blood shed for you for the forgiveness of sins," she knew that the blood of Jesus gives life spiritually. This great blood transfusion is available to all who, by faith, accept our Lord's unconditional love with His **Divine IF.**

Now let me call attention to two additional **ifs** in chapter 2 of I John. In verse 1, we read:

> *"My little children, I am writing this to you so that you*
> *may not sin; but **if** any one does sin, we have an*
> *advocate with the Father, Jesus Christ the righteous."*

Someone may suggest that on the basis of this verse one can "sin bravely" because Jesus is our advocate. Did not Jesus say to the woman taken in adultery, whom the scribes and Pharisees wanted to stone, *"Neither do I condemn you; go and do not sin again."* (John 8:11).

And there is another "**if**" in verse 3 of chapter 2 of St. John's epistle:

> *"And by this we may be sure that we know him,*
> ***if** we keep his commandments."*

Surely, those who try to get rid of the commandments, or tone them down, or rationalize them, or call them the ten suggestions, or say they are out-of-date, have never known Jesus as Saviour and Lord. This **if**, *"If anyone does sin"* reminds us that we have not only a Saviour who died on the cross, taking our sin and guilt in His own body, but also an advocate with the Father, praying for us at the Father's right hand in glory.

In His High Priestly Prayer, found in John 17:22,23, we read:

> *"The glory which thou hast given me I have given to*
> *them, that they may be one even as we are one, I in them*
> *and thou in me, that they may become perfectly one, so that*
> *the world may know that thou hast sent me and hast*
> *loved them even as thou hast loved me."*

Jesus prayed that He may be in us, His followers, and we may be in Him. This means that we "not okay" persons can be made really okay and completely righteous and more. It means that we are called to share His love with others so that they too find new life in Him. Amazing Grace! We can move from the cross of Calvary to the empty tomb on Easter Sunday morning.

We come back to II Corinthians 5:17:

*"Therefore, **if** any one is in Christ, he is a new creation;*
the old has passed away, behold, the new has come."

This **if** points to the miracle of restoration.

Some time ago, I visited a farm where a large building contained fourteen antique cars. There was an 1899 Locomobile, a 1900 Stanley Steamer, a Buick, several Fords, a Sears Roebuck car and a Maxwell.

The thing that impressed me most was that every car was being renovated, rebuilt and placed in running order. They were being restored for the purpose for which they were created!

The Christian story is more than the gospel of forgiveness and pardon. It is the gospel of **acquittal**. (Read Psalm 32:1-2 and Romans 5:9 and 17). But it is **more**. It is the gospel of **restoration**.

God not only forgave King David. He restored him to be king and ruler of his people. David, the adulterer and murderer—**Restored**! St. Augustine, lost in lust, prayed for by his Mother—**Restored**! Charles Colson, leader of political intrigue and betrayer of trust—**Restored**!

We are restored to membership in God's family. And more. God restores and reinstates us sinners for a great mission in life—**to live for Christ and for others.**

We close this chapter with words from I John 2:23-25:

"No one who denies the Son has the Father.
He who confesses the Son has the Father also.
Let what you heard from the beginning abide in you.
***If** what you heard from the beginning abides in you,*
then you will abide in the Son and in the Father.
And this is what he has promised us, eternal life."

Ah, yes! These **Divine IFs** are a vital and indispensable part of our journey to Eternal Life and the nearer Presence of our Lord and Saviour.

I'M OKAY BECAUSE
CHAPTER THREE
I'M SO LOVED

Dr. Theodore Conrad, in discussing the meaning of so loved, reminded me that so in the Greek comes from the word "houtoes", meaning "in this way". So we read, "God loved the world in this way." How did He love the world? The answer is in John 3:14,15:

"And as Moses lifted up the serpent in the wilderness,
***so** must the Son of man be lifted up,*
that whoever believes in him may have eternal life."

———◆———

If we want to know the highest meaning of the words **so loved**, we must have a clear vision of the cross. And of course those words, **so loved,** are centered in Jesus. For example, in John 15:9 we read:

*"As the Father has loved me, **so** have I loved you;*
abide in my love."

I'M OKAY BECAUSE
I'M SO LOVED

The late E. Stanley Jones, who preached 60,000 sermons on all continents, tells of strange things he found in pulpits as he stood up to preach.

In one pulpit he found a waste paper basket. He thought to himself, "Many sermons should go in before they go over."

In one pulpit he found wads of chewing gum stuck underneath. He thought, "This may represent a maximum activity of the mouth with a minimum activity of the mind."

In one pulpit he found a screwdriver and thought, "Is the main purpose here to keep the ecclesiastical machinery running smoothly?"

Most startling of all was his discovery in one pulpit of a fire extinguisher. I do not recall what he said about this discovery, but it might have been as follows: "God grant that we shall neither quench or grieve the Holy Spirit. Rather, let the fire of the Spirit fall on all who worship in this place."

I can think of some helpful signs that should be found in pulpits.

We would see Jesus.
Not I but Christ whose cross alone can save.
Show us the way.
Good news, not good views.
Love never fails.
Please tell it like He is.

I recall a very negative and distracting moment in one pulpit as I stood up to preach. A huge open Bible took up the entire space of the pulpit desk. I started to remove it to make room for my Bible and notes. I shudder when I think of that Bible going over the edge of the pulpit and landing on the floor with a thud. Hopefully, this was not a way of saying, "Clear the pulpit of the Word of God, and listen now to my words about Him."

There is a verse that should remind many preachers in the pulpit of who they are and what they are there for:

"For what we preach is not ourselves,
but Jesus Christ as Lord,
with ourselves as your servants for Jesus' sake."
II Corinthians 4:5

Another helpful sign in a pulpit might be, "Tell us the old, old story." What story? It's the greatest story ever told!

*"For God **so loved** the world that he gave his only Son,*
that whoever believes in him should not perish
but have eternal life."
John 3:16

So loved. What does **so** mean? Perhaps the dictionary can be helpful at this point.

The word "so" can be used as a reflexive infinitive, like "in such manner". It can indicate a matter of degree, "Why are you so late" or "Why are you so sad". It's a word that can describe consequences, "They were late and and so they did not go". It can be a word that indicates that which is approximate, "He won $50 or so". It can be an exclamation of surprise or challenge, "So what!" It can indicate in very unclear terms how you are, "How are you? So, so." How shall we explain what that word "so" means in **so loved**? There is only one way. We go to the highest authority and to the source of knowledge and truth. We will never get an adequate explanation or definition of **so loved** by brilliant scholars, famous philosophers, well-known psychologists, psychiatrists or authors of great books.

Dr. Theodore Conrad, in discussing the meaning of **so loved**, reminded me that **so** in the Greek comes from the word "houtoes", meaning "in this way". So we read, "God loved the world in this way." How did He love the world? The answer is in John 3:14,15:

"And as Moses lifted up the serpent in the wilderness,
***so** must the Son of man be lifted up,*
that whoever believes in him may have eternal life."

If we want to know the highest meaning of the words **so**

27

loved, we must have a clear vision of the cross. And of course those words, **so loved**, are centered in Jesus. For example:

*"As the Father has loved me, **so** have I loved you;*
abide in my love."
John 15:9

*"Beloved, if God **so loved** us,*
we also ought to love one another."
I John 4:11

So loved! When we have seen the meaning of **so loved** at the cross of our Lord and Saviour, we become aware of a sadly missing note in much preaching today. Grace, God's unconditional and inclusive love for all sinners, is a popular topic. But how can there be an adequate understanding of grace without an awareness of the reality of sin in our lives? How can we understand the meaning of divine mercy unless it is in the context of divine judgment? Walter Barlow, in his book, *God So Loved*, writes about "redemptive judgment."

But the decisive fact to keep before us is not that Christ is our Judge no less than our Saviour, but that He is our Judge in order that He may be our Saviour. The judgment of God is not outside the sphere of grace, but it is at its very heart. The God who was in Christ, reconciling the world unto Himself, could not but judge sin if sin were ever to be fully forgiven, which is an entirely different matter from condoning it. Many a wrong is condoned which is never forgiven. It is simply wiped off the slate as a bad debt, but the alienation between the one wronged and the wrongdoer persists, and on the level of personal relationship the fact that a wrong is condoned may be the very barrier which makes an estrangement permanent. . .

"Forgiveness implies reconciliation, and no true reconciliation ever was made where the last hidden wrong was not fully admitted by the wrongdoer, fully repented of (with all that repentance implies), and fully forgiven."

28

Hopefully, then, we understand that we are **so loved** by judgment and by grace. We sinners are under divine judgment, but also under grace that is greater than our sin. Ours is a bilingual message — judgment and mercy, law and gospel, sin and grace. Jesus is indeed "our judge no less than our Saviour".

I recall an experience in connection with a trip to Canada to attend an International Christian Ashram. I had a group of seventeen persons with me at the airport. Inasmuch as we were in charge of one of the evening presentations, we brought with us some twenty packages and props, some quite large. These were in addition to our personal baggage. Each of these special packages had to be indicated on an individual ticket. Some of our group had already gone to the gate. We had to get them back to show their tickets in order to check all bags. The woman at the desk worked very slowly. She was quite unhappy with our group and baggage. We asked, "Will all of our bags and packages get on the plane?" We shall never forget the answer. She replied loudly, "No, and neither will you!"

We said, "We must be on that plane, whether the bags make it or not. There are two ninety-year-old ladies out there at the gate who are waiting for us. They need us. We have to be together as a group. We have reservations and tickets for this flight."

All our pleading was in vain. The plane took off with half of our group on board and the rest of us making our way from the desk to another airline. This move was to the great relief of the woman at the desk.

What does this story have to do with **"so loved"** and grace? Explaining our plight to another airline official, he swung into swift and decisive action. He said, "We'll get you on a flight which takes another route to your destination." A few hours later we were on the flight and came to our destination in time for the opening service. The point is this: **Grace means a second chance. Grace means a new plan, a new way, a new beginning.** But, in order to receive this "second chance grace", we had to confess that we were remiss and also at fault. We should have arranged to have all of our group with their tickets at the desk. Remission involves a confession of being remiss.

"And he [John the Baptist] came into all the country
about Jordan, preaching the baptism of repentance
for the remission of sins."
LUKE 3:3 KJV

In another book, I have told the story of how my beautiful life partner, Marta, not only lightened my load of guilt, but was God's messenger in helping to remove it completely. In our fifty-five years together in marriage, I often became so deeply involved in parish ministries and in being available to help others that I became insensitive to Marta's needs and the needs of my family. I also spent some thirty years traveling in the USA, Canada and abroad in evangelism missions. This meant that Marta had an extra load of responsibility. I recall on one occasion that I was pouring out my heart to her and confessing my sins of neglect and insensitivity. To my dying day, I will remember her answer as I was pleading, "Please forgive me." She said softly, "There is nothing to forgive." In those words she gave the very heart of the gospel and the meaning of **so loved** and of divine grace. It's all been forgiven. It's all under the blood. It is all washed away.

Max Lucado, in his book, *The Applause of Heaven*, comments on the verse, Ephesians 2:8, 9:

> "For it is by grace you have been saved. . .not by works, so that no one can boast.
>
> "No other world religion offers such a message. All others demand the right performance, the right sacrifice, the right chant, the right ritual, the right seance or experience. Theirs is a kingdom of trade-offs and barterdom. You do this, and God will give you that.
>
> "The result? Either arrogance or fear. Arrogance if you think you've achieved it, and fear if you think you haven't.
>
> "Christ's kingdom is just the opposite. It is a kingdom for the poor. A kingdom where membership is *granted*, not *purchased*. You are placed in God's kingdom. You are 'adopted'. And this occurs not when you do enough, but when you admit you *can't* do enough. You don't earn it; you simply accept it. As a result, you serve, not out of arrogance or fear, but out of gratitude."

The following words of Oswald Chambers, in his book, *My Utmost For His Highest,* may startle us and may turn some people off the moment they hear his sad, drab, negative message about brooding on the tragedy of Calvary. However, I think we need to hear his words as he comments on Galatians 6:14 KJV:

> *"But God forbid that I should glory, save in the cross of our Lord Jesus Christ, by whom the world is crucified unto me, and I unto the world.*

> "If you want to know the energy of God (i.e., the resurrection life of Jesus) in your mortal flesh, you must brood on the tragedy of God. Cut yourself off from prying personal interest in your own spiritual symptoms and consider bare-spirited the tragedy of God, and instantly the energy of God will be in you. 'Look unto Me,' pay attention to the objective Source and the subjective energy will be there. We lose power if we do not concentrate on the right thing. The effect of the Cross is salvation, sanctification, healing, etc., but we are not to preach any of these, we are to preach Jesus Christ and Him crucified. The proclaiming of Jesus will do its own work... We have to concentrate on the great point of spiritual energy—the Cross, to keep in contact with that centre where all the power lies, and the energy will be let loose. In holiness movements and spiritual experience meetings the concentration is apt to be put not on the Cross of Christ, but on the effects of the Cross."

Is this the kind of message our modern society needs? Brooding on the cross? Will this have an appeal to the younger generation of our day? They want to hear about love, indeed about God's love. They want to be affirmed by the good news that they are loved of God and of others. There is no more eloquent affirmation than this, "You are worth dying for."

> *"For the word of the cross is folly to those who are perishing, but to us who are being saved it is the power of God."*
> I CORINTHIANS 1:18

*"That is, God was in Christ reconciling the world to
himself, not counting their trespasses against them,
and entrusting to us the message of reconciliation."*
II Corinthians 5:19

*"Law came in, to increase the trespass;
but where sin increased, grace abounded all the more."*
Romans 5:20

It is my conviction that thinking young people and adults do not have much respect for "easy religion" and "cheap grace". They know that in every area of human life and endeavor in order to be "successful" they have to walk a very narrow road of discipline and self-sacrifice. Oswald Chambers goes on to say: "The centre of salvation is the Cross of Jesus, and the reason it is so easy to obtain salvation is because it cost God so much. The Cross is the point where God and sinful man merge with a crash and the way to life is opened—but the crash is on the heart of God."

I think I can hear a crescendo of youthful voices saying, "I can believe in a God like that, in a God who loves me like that." I think that many thoughtful young persons would like Marta's message, "No Free Ride", taken from her book, *From Grey to Gold*:

"A few years ago I was on a bus heading for downtown Minneapolis. Several people got on the bus at Lake Street. After they were seated, the driver came back and confronted one of them with these words, 'You didn't pay your fare.' I expected the lady to apologize and to explain that she had forgotten to drop the money into the fare box. Instead she said, 'But I'm only going six blocks.' The driver responded in a no-nonsense tone of voice, 'Lady, anybody who rides has got to pay!' And the woman dug into her purse and paid the fare.

I thought how true the words were, 'Anybody who rides has got to pay.'

You have to pay attention and look around you before

you can enjoy the beauties of the blossoming, singing springtime season of the year.

You have to study and think in order to grow as a person.

You have to move out of the easy chair to know the joy of widening horizons and a fuller life.

You have to know the pain of caring to have the joy of helping others.

You have to practice the presence of God in order to know His will and His way.

You have to work at it in order to have a good family life. It doesn't just happen.

You have to give love before you can know friendship in depth.

The scriptural basis for this truth is graphically told in the words, 'Looking to Jesus... who for the JOY that was set before Him endured the cross, despising the shame.' Hebrews 12:2."

When I was serving as Director of Evangelism for my national Church body, the pre-merger Augustana Lutheran Church, I wrote many evangelism tracts. One of them is entitled, *Were You There When They Crucified My Lord?* In answer to the question, "Were You There?" I wrote:

"Today this question is being urgently examined by religious organizations throughout the world. It appears in various forms: 'Who killed Jesus? Was one religious group responsible, or many? Was the Roman Empire? The human race? Who was there?'

"It is encouraging to note that careless pronouncements of blame are being withdrawn. For example, the spurious charge that the Jews of the first century, and of all subsequent centuries, were collectively and exclusively guilty of the death of Jesus of Nazareth, is being re-examined and retracted."

Who was there? Surely God was there. In Philippians 2:6-8 we read these words:

> *"Who, though he was in the form of God, did not count equality with God a thing to be grasped, but emptied himself, taking the form of a servant, being born in the likeness of men. And being found in human form he humbled himself and became obedient unto death, even death on a cross."*

Yes indeed, God was there!

Many others were there—the soldiers, the two criminals crucified with Jesus, the people just standing by watching, the rulers, the centurion and the multitudes of whom we read in Luke, chapter 23:

> *"Two others also, who were criminals, were led away to be put to death with him."*

> *"And the people stood by, watching. . .the rulers scoffed at him. . .the soldiers also mocked him. . ."*

> *"Now when the centurion saw what had taken place, he praised God, and said, 'Certainly this man was innocent!'"*

> *"And all the multitudes who assembled to see the sight, when they saw what had taken place, returned home beating their breasts."*

> *"And all his acquaintances and the women who had followed him from Galilee stood at a distance and saw these things."*

Now we ask the question, "Were **you** there?" Was it "they" or "we"? We find the answer in Isaiah 53:5,6:

> *"But he was wounded for our transgressions, he was bruised for our iniquities. . . All we like sheep have gone astray;*

we have turned every one to his own way;
and the Lord has laid on him the iniquity of us all."

Quoting again from the tract, "Where You There":

"As a member of the human race, have I not gone astray? Am I righteous—without sin? Christ died for all—including me! I was there!

"Do we continue to crucify Him anew through slander, bigotry, prejudice and self-praise? What about the sin of indifference—yours and mine?

"Does our comfortable adjustment to militarism and to the crippling effects of discrimination have anything to do with the crucifixion of our Lord? What about our slowness to become identified with the suffering and heartbreak of our fellowmen?

"And what about *our* poverty—poverty of concern for people across the street and around the world who have not heard that God loves and cares and saves? What about our preoccupation with marginal things that take priority over the 'giving of a cup of cold water' and helping to bind up bleeding wounds? In turning people away without needed love, understanding and help, are we not turning Jesus away? Are we not crucifying Him?"

So loved! Indeed it means taking a long look at the cross.

So loved. **So loved** by whom? Again, we come back to our key verse: *"God **so** loved the world that he gave his only son. . ."*

So loved. We find its meaning in John 15:13,14:

"Greater love has no man than this,
that a man lay down his life for his friends.
You are my friends if you do what I command you."

My friend, John Jurkow, writes about Jesus who knew the ultimate effect of His cross upon untold thousands:

"At the church where I'm a member, during the opening hymn, we turn to face the cross as it is carried to its place of honor at the front; and as the last hymn is being sung, we again face the cross as it is carried to the back.

"Why all this respect for something that represents an instrument of hellish torture? Because that's what the original cross was: one of the most devilish means of execution ever devised. To read a description of the suffering endured by anyone crucified is a blood-chilling experience.

"It's the emblem of supreme, divine love. God is saying He loves us even though we humans put His Son to death in an absolutely horrific manner.

"The cross is the greatest proof of this love which is being evidenced today by all kinds of works of mercy: hospitals, missions, food shelves, nursing homes—the list goes on and on.

"It's all possible because the love of Jesus is coming through lives devoted to Him. 'We love, because he first loved us.' I John 4:19."

God **so loved** the world. Sometimes in my mind and imagination, I see God the Father and Jesus, just before He was to leave His Father's house and His glory-circled throne. He was leaving for this earthly night of suffering and pain. I hear His Father say, "Son, go down there and give them all of my love." And right now, perhaps Jesus is saying to us, "Now, you go and give them all of my love."

The good news of John 3:16, "*God **so loved** the world that he gave his only Son*", can be understood best in the light of I John 3:16:

> "*By this we know love, that he laid down his life for us;*
> *and we ought to lay down our lives for the brethren.*"

Dear Lord, give us the grace of your indwelling Holy Spirit to go and tell others that they are **so loved**! Amen.

I'M OKAY

CHAPTER FOUR

IN CHRIST

From his book, My Utmost For His Highest, Oswald Chambers writes:

"The bedrock of our Christian faith is the unmerited, fathomless marvel of the love of God exhibited on the Cross of Calvary, a love we never can and never shall merit. Paul says this is the reason we are more than conquerors in all these things, super-victors, with a joy we would not have but for the very things which look as if they are going to overwhelm us...

"We are more than conquerors through Him in all these things, not in spite of them, but in the midst of them."

———————

"All this is from God, who through Christ reconciled us to himself and gave us the ministry of reconciliation; that is, God was in Christ reconciling the world to himself, not counting their trespasses against them, and entrusting to us the message of reconciliation."
II Corinthians 5:18,19

I'M OKAY IN CHRIST

W e now come to the word **in.** There are all kinds of uses for that little word **in.** For example, we say, "*in* the room, *in* the envelope, *in* pain, *in* business, *in* politics, the woman *in* red, *in* my opinion, *in* a storm, *in* an hour, *in* various sizes."

Stanley Jones wrote an entire devotional book on the theme, *In Christ.* He tells us that the phrase "**in Christ**" or its equivalent is found 172 times in the New Testament. St. Paul, the greatest interpreter of Christianity, fastens upon this phrase "**in Christ**" and uses it in his epistles 97 times.

Our key verse for this chapter is II Corinthians 5:17:

> "*Therefore, if any one is* **in Christ,** *he is a new creation; the old has passed away, behold, the new has come.*"

As we study this word **in,** we need to think of two other words, "potential" and "possession". In his book, *In Christ,* Stanley Jones comments on these two words. He reminds us of how Jesus said to His disciples, "Receive the Holy Spirit".

> "The Holy Spirit was theirs potentially, but actually the Holy Spirit was not theirs until by surrender and faith they received the Holy Spirit at Pentecost, when 'they were all filled with the Holy Spirit.' Potentiality had become possession. Without that possession they would have lived on a promise, and it is possible to have a promise in your hand and be empty... It is possible to have possessions as a possibility, but the possessions are only possessions when you possess them."

Now use your imagination for a moment. Suppose I am a waiter in a restaurant. You come in and sit down and I say, "Welcome to my restaurant. Here is the menu. Take your time and I'll be back in a few moments." Coming back a few moments later, I hear you say, "I'm ready to order." Then I say, "The food is all there in the menu before you." And you say, "Yes, I know, but I want the food that's described in the menu." "Sir, it's all there. You have it there." You have the food potentially as a possibility in your thoughts but not as a possession. Many persons are trying to live on the menu instead of the meat. They know the words recorded in the Bible but not the Word made Flesh. They are existing on potentialities and promises instead of the actual possession of salvation **in Christ**.

Now what are some of the alternatives to living **in Christ**? You can live in self. You can try to be alive in money, in power, in a cause, in politics, in false gods. But it is a tragic premise to believe that anyone can stay alive in impersonal things. You cannot stay alive by living in a system of ethics. Life is found only **in** a Saviour, a Saviour of persons. You cannot stay alive by rules, not even the Golden Rule. You find life only **in** the Glorious Ruler. His name is Jesus. You cannot stay alive by sermons. You stay alive only by surrendering to a Saviour. You cannot stay alive by living in principles, no matter how high and lofty. You stay alive only through a Person, Jesus. If a baby is crying for its mother you do not say to the child, "I cannot find your mother, but I'll give you the principles of motherhood."

In Romans 8:32 we have these words:

"He who did not spare his own Son but gave him up for us all, will he not also give us all things with him?"

In Christ we find freedom, as we read in John 8:31B,32:

*"If you continue **in** my word, you are truly my disciples, and you will know the truth, and the truth will make you free."*

Are you concerned about hungry and starving persons in the world? In Jesus, you have the answer. He is not only the bread of life but he fed the 5,000. He said to His disciples in Matthew 14:16B:

"You give them something to eat."

Then He provided food for a multitude of hungry persons.

Do you believe that the greatest of these is love and that we need to love one another? Here is the answer:

"Greater love has no man than this,
that a man lay down his life for his friends."
JOHN 15:13

Oswald Chambers, in his book, *My Utmost For His Highest,* writes:

> "The bedrock of our Christian faith is the unmerited, fathomless marvel of the love of God exhibited on the Cross of Calvary, a love we never can and never shall merit. Paul says this is the reason we are more than conquerors in all these things, super-victors, with a joy we would not have but for the very things which look as if they are going to overwhelm us...
>
> "We are more than conquerors through Him *in* all these things, not in spite of them, but in the midst of them."

Are you concerned about people who are carrying heavy burdens? The answer is to come to Him who carries their burdens and yours.

"Come to me, all who labor and are heavy laden,
and I will give you rest. Take my yoke upon you,
and learn from me; for I am gentle and lowly in heart,
and you will find rest for your souls.
For my yoke is easy, and my burden is light."
MATTHEW 11:28-30

Are you concerned about guilt-ridden persons who are being devastated by their guilt feelings? Can anyone take care of this terrible malady better than Jesus? II Corinthians 5:21(TLB):

"For God took the sinless Christ and poured into
him our sins. Then, in exchange,
he poured God's goodness into us."

Jesus gets rid of guilt feelings by getting rid of the guilt!

Are you concerned about lonely persons? Then listen to these words of Jesus:

"I will not leave you desolate;
I will come to you."
JOHN 14:18

Do these promises sound too glib? It's easy to quote Bible verses to persons in need. But when the Divine Promise becomes incarnate in the Divine Friend, Jesus, who is able to meet every need, the promise has transforming power.

"And my God will supply every need of yours
*according to his riches in glory **in Christ Jesus**."*
PHILIPPIANS 4:19

Are you interested in helping to make possible a new world, a world where there is justice and freedom for the oppressed, food for the hungry, hope for the dispossessed and peace in a world where you see the massacres of persons by the millions? Here is the answer. It is our key verse again, II Corinthians 5:17, but with another translation from the New English Bible:

"When anyone is united to Christ,
there is a new world; the old order has gone,
and a new order has already begun."

To be **in Christ** is the best way to help the needy and to help build a better world. Even from our little corner where we say there isn't much we can do, we need to remember that **in Christ**, we are helping to build a better world.

Perhaps some readers will be surprised when I say that we, in the Church, are facing a crisis more dangerous and destructive than most are willing to admit. In fact, the most serious thing about it is that most persons do not recognize the crisis. I call it the "me and my rights crisis". We need to be aware of the awful abuse of human rights in many countries of the world. We need to get involved in Amnesty International and other agencies fighting to liberate millions of persons from torture, slavery, terrible injustice and persecution. But all too often, we in the Church become so absorbed in "my personal rights, prerogatives and prejudices" that the message of reconciliation is lost.

41

There is only one way for reconciliation to happen in the Church. We read about this in II Corinthians 5:17-20:

> *"Therefore, if any one is **in Christ**, he is a new creation; the old has passed away, behold, the new has come. All this is from God, who through Christ reconciled us to himself and gave us the ministry of reconciliation; that is, God was **in Christ** reconciling the world to himself, not counting their trespasses against them, and entrusting to us the message of reconciliation. So we are ambassadors for Christ, God making his appeal through us. We beseech you on behalf of Christ, be reconciled to God."*

Unity in the Church of Jesus Christ does not come by Church unions and mergers. Stanley Jones was a pioneer in the ecumenical movement. His books, *The Christ of the Indian Road* (1925), *The Christ of Every Road* (1930), and *Christ of the Round Table* (1928), could help leaders in the Church today to center their reconciling and unifying efforts in the Lord and Creator of the Church. In his book, *In Christ*, he writes:

> "In a group of Christians say 'Christ' and you are together. Say 'baptism' or 'bishops' or 'church customs' and you are apart. The one fact in Christianity that holds us together is Christ. Show His Spirit in any situation and it is healing. Show some other spirit and it is disruptive. By trial and error we will have to come together around Him—nothing else will work."

We would do well to meditate on the divine revelation found in Colossians 1:16,17:

> *"For in him all things were created,*
> *in heaven and on earth, visible and invisible,*
> *whether thrones or dominions or principalities or*
> *authorities—all things were created through him*
> *and for him. He is before all things,*
> *and in him all things hold together."*

Now we ask, "What does it mean to be **in Christ**?" It means to be in close relationship as we read in John 1:12:

> *"But to all who received him, who believed in his name,*
> *he gave power to become children of God."*

To be **in Christ** means to be "in union with", organic union such as we read about in John 15:5:

> *"I am the vine, you are the branches.*
> *He who abides in me, and I in him,*
> *he it is that bears much fruit. . ."*

To be **in Christ** means to be centered, clearly focused **in Christ**— your whole self, mind, feelings and will.

Your mind—Isaiah 26:3:

> *"Thou dost keep him in perfect peace,*
> *whose mind is stayed on thee. . ."*

Your emotions—I John 4:19:

> *"We love, because he first loved us."*

Your will is also united with Christ—John 15:14:

> *"You are my friends*
> *if you do what I command you."*

But even after all of these words, we cannot understand with our finite minds the meaning of being **in Christ**. Only the Holy Spirit can lift us out of our sinful selves into Christ. This involves a very costly move and response on our part.

I know I cannot make this move by myself, but I believe in the Holy Spirit. He will give me faith that enables me to respond to "God's First Move". He enables me to accept my Lord's acceptance of me. **In Christ** alone do I become worthy of acceptance. The Holy Spirit makes possible for me the ultimate act of self-surrender whereby I can affirm:

"You, Lord, are all I have and you give me all I need;
my future is in your hands."
PSALM 16:5 GNT

Now let us turn to the letter of St. Paul to the Ephesians, chapter one, verses 3-14. Here we find the phrase **in Christ** and **in him** nine times. Verse 13 sums up in an eloquent way the wonder and glory and miracle of being **in Christ:**

> *"Blessed be the God and Father of our Lord Jesus Christ, who has blessed us **in Christ** with every spiritual blessing in the heavenly places, even as he chose us **in him** before the foundation of the world, that we should be holy and blameless before him. He destined us in love to be his sons through Jesus Christ, according to the purpose of his will, to the praise of his glorious grace which he freely bestowed on us in the Beloved. **In him** we have redemption through his blood, the forgiveness of our trespasses, according to the riches of his grace which he lavished upon us. For he has made known to us in all wisdom and insight the mystery of his will, according to his purpose which he set forth **in Christ** as a plan for the fullness of time, to unite all things **in him**, things in heaven and things on earth.*
>
> ***In him,** according to the purpose of him who accomplishes all things according to the counsel of his will, we who first hoped **in Christ** have been destined and appointed to live for the praise of his glory. **In him** you also, who have heard the word of truth, the gospel of your salvation, and have believed **in him**, were sealed with the promised Holy Spirit, which is the guarantee of our inheritance until we acquire possession of it, to the praise of his glory."*

Being **in Christ** means having hope in the midst of despair, having strength and courage in times of crisis and danger. It means being able to go to the Creator who cares much about what is happening to our bodies which are often stricken and impaired. It means going to the Healer and Sustainer in times of illness and pain. Being **in Christ** means being in Life at the time of death and dying. For those who are **in Christ**, death can mean that strange interlude in which our Lord puts us to sleep, and during the sleep He is fashioning a brand-new body without scars or blemish to be enjoyed in all eternity. Being **in Christ** at the time of death means, for example, that we can watch the great ship with a loved one aboard disappear over the horizon. We lament and cry out, "Look, she's gone!" But this is not true. That great ship is just gone from our sight. It is still there, strong and sturdy as ever. And not long after our lament, "Look, she's gone" will come the cry from the farther shore, "Look, she's coming in."

I remember when all members of our family were gathered around Marta shortly before she moved into her Saviour's nearer presence. During the singing of hymns, the reading of scripture and the quoting of her poems, it was very clear to us that it was not an enemy approaching to take our loved one from us. Rather, we heard the footsteps of the Saviour, and we saw Him coming ever closer, reaching out His hand to take her hand and to walk with her right into Paradise. This is what it means to be in Christ at the hour of death. Let us remember the words of Jesus in John 11:25, 26:

> *"I am the resurrection and the life; he who believes in me, though he die, yet shall he live, and whoever lives and believes in me shall never die."*

In her poem, "Winter's Squirrel" taken from her book, *Seen and Unseen*, Marta writes about our Creator coming in person to walk with us.

"Little grey squirrel,
  did the Creator give you
  instinct
  or did he give you memory?

No matter.
You can hop into a snowbank
and pull out

45

an acorn, remnant of last autumn's harvest,
as though you had marked the spot.

Sometimes I look into my own memory's bank
and what I see
gladdens
like a fresh breeze on a summer day,

And sometimes
what I see
thrusts me into a midnight abyss
of regret and sorrow.

Then I remember
I need not walk that way,
for
my Creator came in person,
a man of sorrows and acquainted with grief,
to walk the darkest road of deepest anguish
on my behalf
and in my stead."

Before we close this chapter, we need to hear one more word to live by. To be **in Christ** by a divine act of Amazing Grace means that **Christ is in us.** We read of this in Colossians 1:27:

> *"To them God chose to make known how great among*
> *the Gentiles are the riches of the glory of this mystery,*
> *which is Christ in you, the hope of glory."*

The following story, "You'll Find Jesus", will tell us more about the miracle of Christ **in** you. I've been unable to trace its origin.

"Tomorrow morning," the surgeon began,
"I'll open up your heart. . ."

"You'll find Jesus there," the boy interrupted.
The surgeon looked up, annoyed. "I'll cut your heart open,"
he continued, "to see how much damage has been done. . ."

"But when you open up my heart, you'll find Jesus in there."

The surgeon looked to the parents, who sat quietly. "When I see how much damage has been done, I'll sew your heart and chest back up and I'll plan what to do next."

"But you'll find Jesus in my heart. The Bible says He lives there. The hymns all say He lives there. You'll find Him in my heart."

The surgeon had had enough. "I'll tell you what I'll find in your heart. I'll find damaged muscle, low blood supply, and weakened vessels. And I'll find out if I can make you well."

"You'll find Jesus there too. He lives there."

The surgeon left. He sat in his office, recording his notes from the surgery, "...damaged aorta, damaged pulmonary vein, widespread muscle degeneration. No hope for transplant, no hope for cure. Therapy—painkiller and bed rest. Prognosis— here he paused— death within one year."

He stopped the recorder, but there was more to be said.

"Why?" he asked aloud. "Why did you do this? You've put him here; you've put him in this pain; and you've cursed him to an early death. Why?"

The Lord answered and said, "The boy, My lamb, was not meant for your flock for long, for he is part of My flock, and will forever be. Here, in My flock, he will feel no pain, and will be comforted as you cannot imagine. His parents will one day join him here, and they will know peace, and My flock will continue to grow."

The surgeon's tears were hot, but his anger was hotter. "You created that boy, and you created that heart. He'll be dead in months. Why?"

The Lord answered, "The boy, My lamb, shall return to My flock for he has done his duty. I did not put My lamb with your flock to lose him, but to retrieve another lost lamb."

The surgeon wept.

The surgeon sat beside the boy's bed;
the boy's parents sat across from him.

The boy awoke and whispered, "Did you cut open my heart?"

"Yes," said the surgeon.

"What did you find?" asked the boy.
"I found Jesus there," said the surgeon.

It's a good place to find Jesus. If you find Him there, you will find Him everywhere. We need to pray the words of a hymn:

"Into my heart, into my heart,
    Come into my heart, Lord Jesus,
Come in today, Come in to stay,
    Come into my heart, Lord Jesus.

"Rule in my heart, rule in my heart,
    Thou King of my heart, Lord Jesus,
Make this Thy throne, Rule there alone,
    Thou King of my heart, Lord Jesus.

"Walking with Thee, walking with Thee,
    We're walking with Thee, Lord Jesus,
In work, in play, We serve, we pray,
    We're walking with Thee, Lord Jesus."

I'M OKAY

CHAPTER FIVE

BY FAITH

Here is a **perspective of faith** in the midst of bombings and brokenness. The Christian faith finds its expression, not only in worship, not only in the Church, but primarily outside the walls of the Church and in the world, in the midst of controversial issues of the day. Therefore, I pose the question, "What does my faith have to do with the Oklahoma City bombing, with the bomber, Timothy McVeigh, and with capital punishment?" The answer lies in another execution. This was the execution of Jesus Christ in Jerusalem two thousand years ago.

———◆———

"Surely he has borne our griefs and carried our sorrows;
yet we esteemed him stricken, smitten by God, and
afflicted. But he was wounded for our transgressions,
he was bruised for our iniquities;
upon him was the chastisement that made us whole,
and with his stripes we are healed"
ISAIAH 53:4,5

I'M OKAY BY FAITH

Words are important. And it is indeed important for us to know the meaning of words that we use. Are the words, "my God", profanity, or are they prayer? Do we really believe that words can kill lives or save lives? Are we careless about remarks that can leave scars in somebody's life forever? Do we realize that a word of encouragement and affirmation can bring new life and hope to someone in desperate need?

Let me share a poem from my wife Marta's book of narrative verse, *Seen and Unseen*. The title is "Theft".

> "There are those who steal silver and gold,
>   and there are those who steal
>   the most precious commodity of all—
>   the life of another.
>
> Not with gun,
>   nor with axe,
>   but with words
>   and with scorn.
>
> They diminish life bit by bit,
>   robbing another
>   of tranquillity
>   and joy
>   and dignity,
>   by complaining,
>   demeaning,
>   scolding,
>   mocking,
>   nagging.
>
> Their name, too, is 'Thief'."

From this we realize it is not difficult to become a thief, one who steals joy by the words that we use. Do we specialize in words of complaint or praise? I read these words, "Lament or Praise", in a newsletter entitled, *Silver Strands,* edited by Lucille Erickson:

"Today I can feel sad that I don't have more money OR I can be glad that my finances encourage me to plan my purchases wisely and guide me away from waste. Today I can lament over all that my parents didn't give me when I was growing up OR I can feel grateful that they allowed me to be born. Today I can mourn my lack of friends OR I can excitedly embark upon a quest to discover new relationships. Today I can whine because I have to go to work OR I can shout for joy because I have a job to do. Today I can murmur dejectedly because I have to do housework OR I can feel honored because the Lord has provided shelter for my mind and for my body and for my soul. Shall we use words of complaint or words of gratitude and praise?"

The Bible reminds us of idle words and of words that condemn us:

"I tell you, on the day of judgment men will render account for every careless word they utter; for by your words you will be justified, and by your words you will be condemned."
MATTHEW 12:36,37

In contrast, we wish to highlight life-giving words—words to live by. The word for this chapter is **by**, but as readers have discovered, our two-letter words are never used alone.

We turn to the scriptures to enlighten us on the term, **by faith**.

*"Behold, he whose soul is not upright in him shall fail, but the righteous shall live **by his faith**."*
HABAKKUK 2:4

*"But my righteous one shall live **by faith**, and if he shrinks back, my soul has no pleasure in him."*
HEBREWS 10:38

*"And he made no distinction between us and them, but cleansed their hearts **by faith**."*
ACTS 15:9

51

Our key verse is found in Galatians 2:20:

> *"I have been crucified with Christ; it is no longer I who*
> *live, but Christ who lives in me; and the life I now live*
> *in the flesh I live **by faith** in the Son of God,*
> *who loved me and gave himself for me."*

By faith. As we begin it is important for us to ask the question, "What is faith?" St. Paul gives us one definition in Hebrews 11:1:

> *"Now faith is the assurance of things hoped for,*
> *the conviction of things not seen."*

If we continue in that chapter, we see how the great men of God in the Old Testament lived and worked and suffered **by faith**. In John 11:40 we learn that **believing is seeing**. Jesus said to Martha at the grave of her brother Lazarus:

> *"Did I not tell you that if you would believe*
> *you would see the glory of God?"*

In John 4:11,13,14, we read the story about the Samaritan woman at the well. She was amazed that Jesus was speaking to her, a Samaritan. She had come to draw water from the well. We quote:

> *"The woman said to him, 'Sir, you have nothing to draw*
> *with, and the well is deep; where do you get that living*
> *water'. . . Jesus said to her, 'Every one who drinks of this*
> *water will thirst again, but whoever drinks of the water*
> *that I shall give him will never thirst; the water that I*
> *shall give him will become in him a spring of water*
> *welling up to eternal life.'"*

Let us hear what Oswald Chambers writes about this passage in his book, *My Utmost for His Highest*. "Jesus does not bring anything up from the wells of human nature. . . We impoverish His ministry the moment we forget He is Almighty; the impoverishment is in us, not in Him. We will come to Jesus as

Comforter or as Sympathizer, but we will not come to Him as Almighty."

Indeed, Jesus had nothing to draw with. Indeed, the well was very deep, but Jesus does not bring the living water from down below. He brings it from above. So the question comes to us, "Do we believe, as the Samaritan woman came to believe, Jesus' words? And thereby do we know with blessed assurance that we have an Almighty God?

We often hear the question, "What do you believe?" A more important question is, "In Whom do you believe?" or "Whom do you trust?" We now consider the meaning of faith in the Triune God.

By faith in God the Father. "I believe in God the Father Almighty, Creator of heaven and earth." In my evening devotions and late night walk, I meditate on God my Father. It is indeed overwhelming for me to think that I, a sinner, can come into His holy presence and say, "God, my Heavenly Father, my Creator and Sustainer, Source of all power, majesty, glory, might, honor, blessing, holiness, salvation, righteousness, grace, mercy and peace, the Source of every good and perfect gift." This is a deep experience of the wonder and glory of who He is.

By faith in God the son. "I believe in Jesus Christ, His only Son, our Lord." I remember what Martin Luther said about Jesus in his explanation of the second article of the creed.

> "I believe that Jesus Christ, true God, begotten of the Father from eternity, and also true man, born of the Virgin Mary, is my Lord, who has redeemed me, a lost and condemned creature, secured and delivered me from all sins, from death and the power of the devil, not with silver and gold, but with His holy and precious blood, and with His innocent sufferings and death, in order that I might be His own, live under Him in His kingdom and serve Him in everlasting righteousness, innocence and blessedness, even as He is risen from the dead, and lives and reigns to all eternity. This is most certainly true."

This powerful revelation of who Jesus is, and what He has

done calls for a rising crescendo of praise, "Mine eyes have seen the glory of the coming of the Lord. Glory, Hallelujah!"

By faith in God the Spirit. "I believe in the Holy Spirit." What do we mean by this confession? It means that we are willing to surrender our very lives for the gift of the presence of Jesus as ruler and guide. I Corinthians 12:3B gives us an eloquent reminder:

> "...no one can say 'Jesus is Lord'
> except by the Holy Spirit."

Power for Christian witness comes from the Holy Spirit as we read in Acts 1:8A:

> "But you shall receive power when the Holy Spirit
> has come upon you; and you shall be my witnesses..."

Living **by faith** means that we will be living witnesses in His world. It means that we are willing to become active in Jesus' work of healing and reconciliation in our sin-cursed world. But it means more. We have a prerequisite in John 3:3:

> "...Truly, truly, I say to you, unless one is born anew,
> he cannot see the kingdom of God."

I believe that I received the new birth, my second birth, when Jesus came to live within me in my baptism. Then I became His redeemed child, a member of His kingdom. I received forgiveness of my sins, new life in Christ, my Saviour. I was nurtured in the faith so that I could come to a conscious acceptance of Jesus' acceptance of me, and to a conscious acknowledgement of Jesus as my Saviour and Lord. So for me it takes the new birth, being born of water and the Spirit to enable me to enter the Kingdom of God as His redeemed child. It takes the new birth for me to see the wonder and glory of the Kingdom of God. It is a very important part of my faith to say and affirm with all of my heart, "I believe in the Holy Spirit."

To study the roots of our faith is important, but the fruit of our faith, the fruit of the Spirit, will reveal whether or not we are grounded in divine revelation.

"But the fruit of the Spirit is love, joy, peace, patience, kindness, goodness, faithfulness, gentleness, self-control."
GALATIANS 5:22,23A

Faith reveals treasure. Let me take you on a treasure hunt in Bermuda. Bermuda is one of the unique islands of the world. It is an isolated speck of land in the Atlantic Ocean, covering just under 21 square miles and located 763 miles southeast of New York. The island is thought to have been created by volcanic activity with most of the rock now under water and covered by coral reefs. Through the past four centuries, over 300 ships have been wrecked upon the dangerous underwater, rock-bound reefs. These wrecks in watery graves are a boon and challenge to modern divers. Fabulous Spanish and Portuguese treasures have been discovered in recent years. In the summer of 1968, gold jewelry, ingots, a coin hoard and priceless artifacts have come to light.

The island has no rivers or streams and must depend entirely on rain for water. Every home and building has a thick slate roof, in terraced pyramid form. Rain runs down the ridges and gutters into underground tanks. The roofs are painted white. Bermuda from the air is a sea of gleaming roofs. A lime coating on roofs and in water tanks helps keep the rain water pure. With confidence we drink rain water on our visits there. During a drought, they use distillation plants to transform ocean water into drinking water. A Salvation Army officer told us that the two favorite songs there are, "Fill My Cup, Lord" and "Fill My Tank, Lord!"

While attending twenty-seven Ashram sessions, speaking thirteen times, and leading six devotional periods, I did find time one afternoon at one of our annual Ashrams in Bermuda to make a journey to the southern tip of the island by motorbike. Motorbiking there is exhilarating and bewildering. As I drove along, I had to remember three things: 1) keep left; 2) slow down in the traffic of small cars and motorbikes; 3) hug the edge of the narrow road on curves. I was so busy with these three things that I missed much of the beauty of the magnificent landscape. I decided to walk around the ancient and historic fort. Meeting a couple coming from the other direction, I asked, "Can you please tell me where I am going?" The man replied, "We just came from there and we don't know where it was." Lacking a sense of direction and guidance, I'm sure I missed some treasures.

This travelogue should serve as a reminder that there are treasures at the bottom of the ocean, treasures from the sky in the form of rain and treasures on land everywhere on that beautiful island.

But in Bermuda we found the greatest treasure in all the world, fabulous and magnificent beyond all human reckoning. It's the treasure of God's Word—the treasures of His Book. We met Jesus, the priceless Treasure, the Pearl of great price. And we saw Him bring treasures up and out of ship-wrecked lives.

There's treasure for us right here—right where we are. Look in the Book. In II Corinthians 4:7 (TLB) we read:

"But this precious treasure—this light and power
that now shine within us—is held in a perishable
container, that is, in our weak bodies.
Everyone can see that the glorious power
within must be from God and is not our own."

There's treasure hidden in your God-created life. Amidst the shipwreck, amidst the blasted hopes and spoiled lives right here—amidst the lonely ones who feel unneeded and unwanted—amidst the doubting ones and the sorrowing, there is great treasure. As we open our lives to God in faith we will find it! Treasure indeed! The treasure of forgiveness and new life in Jesus Christ. The treasure of the Holy Spirit—Jesus' indwelling Presence. God's treasure for you!

Here is a **perspective of faith** in the midst of bombings and brokenness. The Christian faith finds its expression, not only in worship, not only in the Church, but primarily outside the walls of the Church and in the world, in the midst of controversial issues of the day. Therefore, I pose the question, "What does my faith have to do with the Oklahoma City bombing, with the bomber, Timothy McVeigh, and with capital punishment?" The answer lies in another execution. This was the execution of Jesus Christ in Jerusalem two thousand years ago.

He was the only perfect man who ever lived in our world. He

suffered the cruelest, most torturous kind of death ever invented by humans as they tried to destroy one they called their enemy. In reality, He was the best Friend, Protector and Saviour they could ever have.

In just six hours of excruciating pain, Jesus bore in His divine-human body all the suffering, pain, shock, terror, loss and torture of spirit that victims and their families in the Oklahoma City bombing experienced. And more. He took in His body and spirit all the sins, violence, murders, grief, hopelessness and despair that could be felt by us humans. He bore the sins of all persons of all time from the beginning of the world, even the sins of Timothy McVeigh who died in his sins as he refused to turn to the cross and watch Jesus die for him.

It is impossible for me to walk in the shoes of the victims and their families who came out of the bombing catastrophe with scarred lives and broken hopes. Indeed, I cannot possibly comprehend their pain and indescribable terror. In my 91 years I have suffered loss and heavy burdens in which only the Divine Burden-bearer could sustain and rescue me. But never have I experienced what they went through and are still enduring today.

But my faith takes me beyond Oklahoma City and the death chamber in Terre Haute, Indiana. I see the place of another explosion, yes, and the place of another execution. There was a terrifying clash between good and evil, between Satan who inspires hate and our God who brings love. Indeed, He is love. Jesus, His Son, died a tortuous death in this clash. The Christian faith affirms that Jesus, the world's only truly innocent man, died for all sinners. The choice before us is to respond either with our human emotions of hate and revenge or with faith in the transforming Word of the Friend who gave His life for us.

He is the cure for sin-sickness, and not for ours only but for that of the whole world:

"My children, in writing this to you my purpose is that you
should not commit sin. But should anyone commit a sin,
we have one to plead our cause with the Father,
Jesus Christ, and he is just."
I JOHN 2:1 NEB

"Surely he has borne our griefs and carried our sorrows;
yet we esteemed him stricken, smitten by God, and
afflicted. But he was wounded for our transgressions,
he was bruised for our iniquities;
upon him was the chastisement that made us whole,
and with his stripes we are healed."
ISAIAH 53:4,5

Of course, some will affirm that McVeigh's crime was so heinous (168 victims dying terrifying deaths, including 19 children) that the bomber's execution was the only justifiable punishment. The alternate punishment would be life imprisonment without parole. This would be a far more severe punishment than the "comfortable" death he experienced. Will his ghost bring to an end all bitter memories?

And is it possible that this stone-hearted man, bloody but unbowed, apparently basking in his public limelight, defiant, the killer of babies for his personal satanic cause, could repent and be saved for eternal life with God whom he defied? During His agony on the cross, Jesus said to a repentant criminal being crucified beside Him, "Today, you shall be with me in paradise."

Charles Colson, founder of Prison Fellowship, can tell us of murderers in prison for life who confessed their sins and crimes before Almighty God. They have believed in the Lamb of God who has taken away all of their sins. They have received divine pardon. They have been transformed into new persons in Christ. After life in prison, they will inherit eternal life.

If I did not believe in the possibility of any sinner being saved by faith in the crucified and risen Saviour, I would have to despair of my own salvation. The Bible says that to hate anyone is murder in the sight of God, in spirit if not in act. This is indeed a sobering thought. I pray that no one who has suffered greatly at the hands of another will self-destruct by the spirit of revenge. What does the Bible say about someone who says, "I will never forgive him?"

"But if you do not forgive men their trespasses,
neither will your Father forgive your trespasses."
MATTHEW 6:15

A man riding on a bus noticed that the man next to him was reading the Bible. He said, "Are you reading about your God in that book?" He received a quiet affirmative reply. Then the man shouted at him, "Where was that good God of yours when my boy died in the war?" The man with the Bible said softly, "I think that he was watching His own Son die!

Indeed, someone may ask, "Where was your loving God when the bomb exploded? Where was he when six million Jews were massacred during World War II?

A dramatic answer was found during my visit to the Oklahoma City Memorial. Visiting the memorial was one of the most sobering times in my life. Among the many tourists there, one heard very little conversation. We walked around in an atmosphere of reverence out of respect for the 168 victims. Seeing those 168 vacant chairs would rule out light-hearted banter. When I saw the special walls dedicated to the children, and the inscriptions and pictures and words drawn by children, it was a time for tears.

When I crossed the street from the Memorial, I saw the most impressive sight of all. The Catholic Church had erected a large statue of Jesus on the lawn. I shall never forget seeing that eloquent tear coming down His face.

Where indeed was God that tragic day? He was watching His beloved Son die. And more. I believe that the earthquake that shook the world as Jesus was dying on the cross might have been the sobs of the Father as He made no answer to Jesus' cry, "My God, my God, why have You forsaken me?"

He had created a perfect world. The devil enticed our first parents to doubt what God had said. They had been created with free will. This is a magnificent gift. Without it, we would be puppets and automatons. Free will means that I have a moral choice. I can destroy or I can save. With the fall into sin came suffering, disease, tragedies, wars, hatred and revenge, sorrow, loss and death.

But as the plowshare was drawn over paradise, the Garden of Eden turned into a shambles, and the heavenly pair banished to outer darkness, our Father-Creator announced His plan to redeem His lost world. It was the way of the cross, the way of the

59

greatest manifestation of self-giving love this world will ever see. We read of this redemptive plan in Genesis 3:15, in the words of God to the serpent:

"I will put enmity between you and the woman,
and between your seed and her seed;
he shall bruise your head, and you shall bruise his heel."

Can the human spirit survive the atrocities, torture and violence that we hear and read about? The answer is, "No"; the human spirit cannot get through to victory and peace. But filled with the Holy Spirit and **by faith** in a God and in a Saviour who suffer with us, and who give us the victory that overcomes the world, we can not only survive but also affirm with confidence the promise in I John 5:4B:

". . .and this is the victory that overcomes
the world, our faith."

The life of Corrie tenBoom is a remarkable example. She and her sister, together with countless others, were abused, debased and tortured in body and spirit in a concentration camp. Her sister, Betsey, died a slow, torturous death. Corrie survived and became a flaming evangelist for her Lord and Saviour in whom her faith, and her sister's, never wavered. Her message across the world was that in Jesus Christ, good conquers evil and that in the hearts of believers, faith in the promises of God makes of us more than conquerors. Here are some of those promises:

"I can do all things in him who strengthens me."
PHILIPPIANS 4:13

"For I am sure that neither death, nor life, nor angels,
nor principalities, nor things present, nor things to come,
nor powers, nor height, nor depth, nor anything else in
all creation, will be able to separate us from the love of God
in Christ Jesus our Lord."
ROMANS 8:38,39

Before Corrie's death in 1983, a nurse who had been especially cruel to her sister, Betsey, was in an audience where Corrie was speaking. In her book, *Oh, How He Loves You*, Corrie uses the story of her meeting with this nurse as a teaching lesson on forgiveness to a friend in a hospital. On a visit Corrie saw that she was very ill. She also noticed an expression of bitterness on her face. As they talked, she told Corrie about her husband.

"I know that I will be ill for a long time. The doctor does not give me any hope that I can do my work for a long time to come. My husband did not like having a sick wife. He left me and now lives with a younger woman. He never comes to see me."

"Have you forgiven him?"

"No, I certainly have not!"

"I will tell you something of my own experiences, when I felt bitter about someone. It was in Germany. One day I saw a lady in a meeting who did not look into my eyes. Suddenly I recognized her. She was a nurse who had been very cruel to my dying sister when we were in Ravensbruck concentration camp during the war. When I saw her, a feeling of bitterness, almost hatred, came into my heart. How my dying sister had suffered because of her! The moment I felt that hatred in my heart, I knew that I myself had no forgiveness. It was the Lord Jesus who said to us, 'If ye forgive not men their trespasses, neither will your Father forgive your trespasses' (Matt. 6:15).

"I knew I had to forgive her, but I could not. Then I had a good talk with the Lord about it when I was at home later. 'Lord, you know I cannot forgive her. My sister suffered too much because of her cruelties. I know, Lord, that I must forgive, but I cannot.' Then the Lord gave me, 'The love of God is shed abroad in our hearts by the Holy Spirit which is given unto us' (Rom. 5:5).

"The Lord taught me a prayer: 'Thank You, Lord, for Romans 5:5. Thank You, Jesus that You brought into my heart God's love by the Holy Spirit who is given to me.

Thank You, Father, that Your love in me is stronger than my hatred and bitterness.' The same moment I knew I could forgive.

"I told a friend about my experience and she said, 'Oh, I know that nurse. She works in a hospital not far from here.'

"Can you call her?"

"Sure I can." She called the nurse, and I had a talk with her over the telephone, telling her that when I had the next meeting that evening, I would have a different message and would very much like her to come.

"Her answer was, 'You would like to see *me* in your meeting?'

"Yes, that is why I phoned. I should like it very much."

"Then I will come." She did come, and during the entire evening she looked into my eyes while I spoke. After the meeting, I had a talk with her. I told her that I had been bitter, but that God's Holy Spirit in me had brought His love instead of hatred and that now I loved her. I told her that it was through Jesus Christ who bore our sins on the cross. He forgave us, but He also fills our hearts with God's love through the Holy Spirit, and that is why I could invite her to come to the second meeting.

I told her more, and at the end of our talk that nurse accepted the Lord Jesus Christ as her personal Savior and Lord. Do you see the miracle? I, who had hated her, was used by God to bring her to the acceptance of Jesus Christ. Not only will the Lord cleanse us by His blood, but He will also use us. He used me, who hated her, and God had so absolutely forgiven and cleansed *me* that He could use me to show *her* the way of salvation!

"You are bitter about your husband, but claim Romans 5:5. I know that you love the Lord Jesus. You have known Him for a long time. Trust Him to do the miracle of bringing into your heart so much of God's love that you can forgive your husband!" I prayed with her and left.

A week later I was once more in her room. When I saw her, I knew that God had done something in her heart. "I am absolutely free. The Lord has done in me such a tremendous miracle that I could forgive my husband. You know, now there is a great peace and joy in me."

"Yes, we never touch the ocean of God's love so much as when we love our enemies. It is a joy to *accept* forgiveness, but it is almost a greater joy to *give* forgiveness."

> *"The love of God is shed abroad in our hearts*
> *by The Holy Ghost which is given unto us."*
> ROMANS 5:5B (KJV)

Do we wish to change things for the better? Do we believe that change is possible? Does anyone believe that hate is better than love? In her book, *From Grey to Gold*, Marta Berg wrote these eloquent lines in her poem, "A Maid and a Carpenter":

"Do you know what I want to be when I grow up?'
It was a four-year-old's question.
'No. What?'
'A maid, cause then I can make everything
in the world
sparkly clean.'

Her brothers quickly disillusioned her.
They gave a recital of the hard realities
of low pay and onerous work.

Because of two little boys
the world lost its chance to become 'sparkly clean.'

But a man was sent to earth
with a plan and with power,
awesome power
to sweep clean every human heart,
priest and publican alike.
That one who changed the world was a carpenter.
Even now He has the power to change the world
or to change one life.

You and I can know this power.
LOVE is its name."

In 1974, I stood in the pulpit of a beautiful new church building in Hiroshima, Japan. It had been erected on the site of the church that was destroyed when our atomic bomb exploded, killing nearly all of the church members. Over 100,000 others suffered tortuous deaths. I visited the museum and saw faces of men, women and children melted into blobs of human flesh. These had no part in the "act of infamy" at Pearl Harbor in which our American service men and women were blown up in their ships and barracks.

I visited a hospital where I saw the scarred and mutilated faces and emaciated bodies of survivors still suffering from the lethal and poisoned air.

Later, as I stood at the memorial site at the center of the explosion, I was called on to speak for the American group. Before me stood Pastor Tanimota whose church and congregation had been destroyed. This was one of the most moving moments of my life. My prayer was a cry from my heart. "God have mercy upon us. God have mercy upon Japan. God have mercy upon the USA. God have mercy upon the Church." We prayed, "Never again a Pearl Harbor murderous attack. Never again an atomic bomb explosion."

Is "never again" a possibility? I believe that we in the Church have the answer. If millions of us in the Church, by the power of the cross and by the power of His resurrection, let Him change our lives and life styles and fill us with His love, then millions outside the Church will be changed. Evil will be with us in this fallen, sin-cursed world. Terrorism will be a reality, suffering and pain will continue and physical death will be our earthly destiny. But in the midst of it all, as co-workers with Christ in His work of healing and reconciliation in the world, we will help many weary and struggling travelers make it safely to the Promised Land.

Now I ask this question. Do you believe in Jesus' promise when He says in John 14:18:

"I will not leave you desolate; I will come to you."

And do you believe in the promise in Psalm 50:15?

"And call upon me in the day of trouble;
I will deliver you, and you shall glorify me."

Do you believe that He will come in the midst of your sorrow, physical impairments, pain, sense of loss and loneliness, your heavy burden of guilt, your longing for things to be different in this life? Perhaps you are longing to be released to go Home. Do you believe that He comes to you, that He will always come and that He is here? I have one final illustration which hopefully will explain in a real life situation the meaning of John 14:18.

This is a story from World War I. It's a story of a young lad in a trench. There had been shooting at the enemy and gunfire from the enemy that had killed all but two or three of the Americans. There was one American out there in no-man's land severely wounded. In a trench on the American side there was a lieutenant and a private. The private said, "I've got to go over and help my buddy. I've got to try to bring him here. I know him." The lieutenant says, "You can't go. You can't make it. You'll be killed! I command you not to go." But that young man climbed out of the trench, crawled on his stomach to his friend, and pulled and dragged him back into the trench. Just as he was about to fall over to the bottom of the trench with his friend, he was hit by a bullet, and that young man lay at the bottom of the trench dying. The lieutenant reminded him that his buddy was already dead, so he said to the private, (he must have been a very insensitive person), "I told you you shouldn't have gone. Look at you. Your buddy is dead and you are dying. I told you it wouldn't be worth it." "Oh," said the young man with his dying words, "Oh, yes, yes, sir. It was worth it because when I came to my buddy I heard him say, 'I knew you'd come. I knew you'd come.'"

I hope that this is the faith we live by. I know He will come. I know that He is here. May we know that our Lord and Saviour is here. We will know it **by faith**, by personal experience, by a sense of His presence. And then I believe we can sing this song together:

"All the way my Saviour leads me;
What have I to ask beside?

Can I doubt His tender mercy,
Who thro' life has been my Guide?

Heav'nly peace, divinest comfort,
Here by faith in Him to dwell!

For I know, whate'er befall me,
Jesus doeth all things well.

"All the way my Saviour leads me;
O the fullness of His love!

Perfect rest to me is promised
In my Father's house above.

When my spirit, clothed immortal,
Wings its flight to realms of day,

This my song through endless ages:
Jesus led me all the way."

It is a costly faith as we are reminded in Galatians 3:20:

"I have been crucified with Christ; it is no longer I who live, but Christ who lives in me; and the life I now live in the flesh I live by faith in the Son of God, who loved me and gave himself for me."

Live your faith here and now. Die in the faith and live forever!

BECAUSE GOD IS,
CHAPTER SIX
I CAN BE OKAY

From his book, *The Great House of God,* Max Lucado writes:

"Now as you stand in the observatory viewing God's workshop, let me pose a few questions. If he is able to place the stars in their sockets and suspend the sky like a curtain, do you think it remotely possible that God is able to guide your life? If your God is mighty enough to ignite the sun, could it be that he is mighty enough to light your path? If he cares enough about the planet Saturn to give it rings or Venus to make it sparkle, is there an outside chance that he cares enough about you to meet your needs?"

———————

"Have you not known? Have you not heard?
The Lord is the everlasting God, the Creator of the
ends of the earth. He does not faint or grow weary,
his understanding is unsearchable. He gives power to the
faint, and to him who has no might he increases strength."
Isaiah 40:28,29

BECAUSE GOD IS,
I CAN BE OKAY ⚜

The story is told of a novice in a religious order who was assigned by his superior to give a homily at the seminary chapel service. As he appeared before his fellow students, his hands trembled, his knees shook and his mouth was dry as he began his talk. He said, "Does anyone know what I am going to say this morning?" No hands went up. He continued, "Neither do I. Let us stand for the benediction." His superior reprimanded him severely and instructed him to study and prepare to speak the following day. He came to the meeting, and once again his knees shook, his voice trembled and he perspired heavily. He said, "Does anyone know what I am going to say?" All hands went up. He continued, "Then I don't need to tell you what you already know. Let us stand for the benediction." He was called into the office of his superior who threatened him with expulsion unless he fulfilled his assignment on the following day. Again he appeared in the same physical condition. He said, "Will those who know what I am going to say raise their hands?" Many hands went up. He continued, "Will those who do not know what I am going to say, please raise your hands." Again many hands went up. The novice then said, "Let those who know tell those who do not know. Let us stand for the benediction."

Now let me ask this question of my readers. Do any of you know what I am going to say about God and who **He is**? If you do I would suggest that you read no further. I would not want to waste your time by telling you what I know about God.

Can any of us really know who **God is**? Yes, on two conditions: 1) By believing what God says about Himself and, 2) By believing in God's highest revelation of Himself in Jesus.

In John 14:6, we read the words of Jesus:

> *"I am the way, and the truth, and the life;*
> *no one comes to the Father, but by me."*

In verse 8, Philip, one of the disciples, says to Jesus:

> *"Lord, show us the Father,*
> *and we shall be satisfied."*

In verse 9, Jesus said to him:

> *"Have I been with you so long,*
> *and yet you do not know me, Philip?*
> *He who has seen me has seen the Father;*
> *how can you say, 'Show us the Father'?"*

In other words, we can never know the truth about our God and Creator unless we know His Son, Jesus Christ, as our Lord and Saviour. Hopefully, readers will now understand why I say this book is not worth reading if all I talk about is who I think God is and what He does. But I have good news for you, so keep reading, remembering that spiritual things are spiritually discerned. I am reassured by the words in John 16:13:

> *"When the Spirit of truth comes, he will guide you into all*
> *the truth; for he will not speak on his own authority,*
> *but whatever he hears he will speak, and he will*
> *declare to you the things that are to come."*

I recall learning in my confirmation class long ago that God is Spirit with all the highest perfections, eternal, unchangeable, all-wise, omnipresent, omnipotent, omniscient, holy and the list goes on and on.

Here is a list of divine attributes that may be of help to readers as they become involved in the study of who **God is**:

> *"Let your light so shine before men,*
> *that they may see your good works and give glory*
> *to your **Father** who is in heaven."*
> **Father** —MATTHEW 5:16

> *"The eternal God is your **dwelling place**,*
> *and underneath are the everlasting arms. . ."*
> **Dwelling Place** —DEUTERONOMY 33:27

*"Behold, God is **mighty**, and does not despise any;*
*he is **mighty** in strength of understanding."*
Mighty —JOB 36:5

*"God is our refuge and **strength**,*
a very present help in trouble."
Strength —PSALM 46:1

"Behold, God is my salvation; I will trust, and will not be
*afraid; for the Lord God is my strength and my **song**,*
and he has become my salvation."
Song —ISAIAH 12:2

"Have you not known? Have you not heard?
*The Lord is the everlasting God, the **Creator** of the ends*
of the earth. He does not faint or grow weary, his
understanding is unsearchable. He gives power to the
faint, and to him who has no might he increases strength."
Creator —ISAIAH 40:28,29

*"God is a **righteous judge**,*
and a judge who has indignation every day."
Righteous Judge —PSALM 7:11

*"The Lord is my **shepherd**, I shall not want."*
Shepherd —PSALM 23:1

*"The Lord is my **light** and my salvation;*
whom shall I fear?"
Light —PSALM 27:1

"Blessed be the Lord who daily bears us up;
*God is our **salvation**."*
Salvation —PSALM 68:19

*"Behold, God is my **helper**;*
the Lord is the upholder of my life."
Helper —PSALM 54:4

*"Extol the Lord our God, and worship at his holy
mountain; for the Lord our God is **holy**!"*
Holy —PSALM 99:9

*"The Lord is your **keeper**;
the Lord is your shade on your right hand."*
Keeper —PSALM 121:5

*"God is **faithful**, by whom you were called into the
fellowship of his Son, Jesus Christ our Lord."*
Faithful —I CORINTHIANS 1:9

*"And God is **able** to provide you with every blessing
in abundance, so that you may always have
enough of everything and may provide in abundance
for every good work."*
Able —II CORINTHIANS 9:8

*"The Lord is **merciful** and gracious,
slow to anger and abounding in steadfast love."*
Merciful —PSALM 103:8

*"Rejoice in the Lord always; again I will say, Rejoice.
Let all men know your forbearance. The Lord is **at
hand**."*
At Hand —PHILIPPIANS 4:4,5

*"For God is **greater than our hearts**,
and he knows everything."*
Greater Than Our Hearts —I JOHN 3:20B

*So we know and believe the love God has for us.
God is **love**, and he who abides in love abides in God,
and God abides in him."*
Love —I JOHN 4:15,16

It is a very difficult assignment for me to choose just a few of
these **"God is"** pictures for additional comment. Hopefully,
readers will use this pictorial directory as a Bible study guide.

GOD IS FATHER

"Let your light so shine before men,
that they may see your good works and give
*glory to your **Father** who is in heaven."*
MATTHEW 5:16

Pastor Marbury Anderson has written a book entitled, *The Lord's Prayer in My Life—the Basic Lessons of Prayer*. This is one of the most helpful and challenging Bible studies on the Lord's Prayer that I have read. In the book he makes this statement about "Father":

> **Father**. The idea of God as Father was not new with Jesus. He simply gave it strong emphasis. Some like to speak of God as the 'Man Upstairs'. Others want to think of God as the 'Great Designer', the 'Supreme Architect of the Universe', the 'Oversoul', the 'Unknowable One', the 'Potentate', and the 'Ruler of the Hearts and Reins of Men'. How impersonal and limited are all these when contrasted with the terminology of Jesus—'Father'. A good parent is one who protects and loves, one who plans and counsels, one who protects and provides. We think of a father as strong, dependable, creative, exemplary, loving, and even stern. God is our Father. By knowing him as our Father we know him as 'thou' or 'you', not 'it'. We also know we are neither displaced persons nor disinherited. We are God's children.

> > "But you have received a spirit of adoption. When we cry, 'Abba! Father!' it is that very Spirit bearing witness with our spirit that we are children of God, and if children, then heirs, heirs of God and joint heirs with Christ—if, in fact, we suffer with him so that we may also be glorified with him. (Romans 8:15b-17)."

I recall a frightening walk in the dark in my childhood. I was eleven or twelve years old and had worked in a potato field all day and evening. When I started my walk to my home in town,

I was enveloped by thick darkness on a lonely road. In my imagination, I heard ominous sounds, and I saw menacing shadows. Suddenly, I heard actual footsteps. I crouched down in a ditch, waiting for the stranger to pass by. Then the sound of steps stopped. I was sure that I was discovered! Was this the end? Then I heard a familiar voice, and my name, "William!" My father had come to meet his frightened little boy! Now we walked together, my hand in his. I was safe and secure.

My father! Our Father! He calls us by name! His hand will never let go.

In her book, *Seen and Unseen*, Marta enlarges upon the thought of God as Father with her poem entitled, "A Word".

"Someone said it,
'God is like Mount Everest,
and I'm a Tonka toy car
trying to get to the top.'

Not So!

Jesus gave us a word,
that puts us in
awesome nearness
to the Creator of the universe,
the Maker of all time and space,
the One whose majesty fills all of
sky and sea and land.

It is a humbling word,
a comforting word,
an unmerited word.

The word is,
'Father'.

God. . .my Father!"

Now let us look at two ***"God is"*** pictures which belong together.

G O D   I S   M I G H T Y   A N D
G O D   I S   S H E P H E R D

*"Behold, **God is mighty**, and does not despise any;*
***he is mighty** in strength of understanding."*
JOB 36:5

*"The **Lord is my shepherd**, I shall not want."*
PSALM 23:1

We turn to Isaiah 40, verses 10 and 11 for a picture of **a mighty God and a gentle Shepherd**:

"Behold, the Lord God comes with might,
and his arm rules for him; behold, his reward is
with him, and his recompense before him. He will
feed his flock like a shepherd, he will gather the lambs
in his arms, he will carry them in his bosom,
and gently lead those that are with young."

There is a description of our Mighty God, Creator of the universe, and the Good Shepherd who carries the lambs in His arms. It is found in a sermon, "Go Down Death", from the book, *God's Trombones*, by James Weldon Johnson.

"Weep not, weep not,
She is not dead;
She's resting in the bosom of Jesus.
Heart-broken husband – weep no more;
Grief-stricken son – weep no more;
Left-lonesome daughter – weep no more;
She's only just gone home.

Day before yesterday morning,
God was looking down from his great, high heaven,
Looking down on all his children,
And his eye fell on Sister Caroline,
Tossing on her bed of pain.
And God's big heart was touched with pity,

74

With the everlasting pity.

And God sat back on his throne,
And he commanded that tall, bright angel standing
    at his right hand:
Call me Death!
And that tall, bright angel cried in a voice
That broke like a clap of thunder:
Call Death! – Call Death!
And the echo sounded down the streets of heaven
Till it reached away back to that shadowy place,
Where Death waits with his pale, white horses.

And Death heard the summons,
And he leaped on his fastest horse,
Pale as a sheet in the moonlight.
Up the golden street Death galloped,
And the hoofs of his horse struck fire from the gold,
But they didn't make no sound.
Up Death rode to the Great White Throne,
And waited for God's command.

And God said: Go down, Death, go down,
Go down to Savannah, Georgia,
Down in Yamacraw,
And find Sister Caroline.
She's borne the burden and heat of the day,
She's labored long in my vineyard,
And she's tired –
She's weary –
Go down, Death, and bring her to me.

And Death didn't say a word,
But he loosed the reins on his pale, white horse,
And he clamped the spurs to his bloodless sides,
And out and down he rode,
Through heaven's pearly gates.
Past suns and moons and stars;
On Death rode,
And the foam from his horse was like a comet in the sky;

On Death rode,
Leaving the lightning's flash behind;
Straight on down he came.

While we were watching round her bed,
She turned her eyes and looked away,
She saw what we couldn't see;
She saw Old Death. She saw Old Death
Coming like a falling star.
But Death didn't frighten Sister Caroline;
He looked to her like a welcome friend.
And she whispered to us: I'm going home,
And she smiled and closed her eyes.

And Death took her up like a baby,
And she lay in his icy arms,
But she didn't feel no chill.
And Death began to ride again –
Up beyond the evening star,
Out beyond the morning star,
Into the glittering light of glory,
On to the Great White Throne.
And there he laid Sister Caroline
On the loving breast of Jesus.

And Jesus took his own hand and wiped away her tears,
And he smoothed the furrows from her face,
And the angels sang a little song,
And Jesus rocked her in his arms,
And kept a-saying: Take your rest,
Take your rest, take your rest.

Weep not – weep not,
She is not dead;
She's resting in the bosom of Jesus."

These two attributes of God, **"mighty God and gentle Shepherd"**, are deeply significant in our faith. Our God **is** almighty, Lord of all creation, Lord of all nations, Lord of history, Lord of life and death. He is the creator of millions of galaxies of stars that cause scientists, even in their narrow glimpses of creation, to marvel. Would that they would bow down before the awesomeness and wonder of it all!

GOD IS CREATOR

"Have you not known? Have you not heard? The Lord *is the everlasting God, the **Creator** of the ends of the earth. He does not faint or grow weary, his understanding is unsearchable. He gives power to the faint, and to him who has no might he increases strength."*
ISAIAH 40:28,29

One of my favorite chapters in the Bible is Isaiah 40. Here I read of our mighty God. This chapter should be read often, especially when doubts assail us about our great God and Saviour.

To enhance this picture of our God, I quote from Max Lucado's book, *The Great House of God*. These paragraphs are taken from a section entitled, "God's Workshop".

> "Behold the sun! Every square yard of the sun is constantly emitting 130,000 horse power, or the equivalent of 450 eight-cylinder automobile engines. And yet our sun, as powerful as it is, is but one minor star in the 100 billion orbs which make up our Milky Way Galaxy. Hold a dime in your fingers and extend it arm's length toward the sky, allowing it to eclipse your vision, and you will block out fifteen million stars from your view.

> "Consider the earth! Our globe's weight has been estimated at six sextillion tons (a six with twenty-one zeroes). Yet it is precisely tilted at twenty-three degrees; any more or any less and our seasons would be lost in a melted polar flood. Though our globe revolves at the rate of one thousand miles per hour or twenty-five thousand miles per day or nine million miles per year, none of us tumbles into orbit. Our God who 'stretches the northern sky out over the empty space and hangs the earth upon nothing' (Job 26:7) also created an invisible band of gravity to hold us secure.

"Now as you stand in the observatory viewing God's workshop, let me pose a few questions. If he is able to place the stars in their sockets and suspend the sky like a curtain, do you think it remotely possible that God is able to guide your life? If your God is mighty enough to ignite the sun, could it be that he is mighty enough to light your path? If he cares enough about the planet Saturn to give it rings or Venus to make it sparkle, is there an outside chance that he cares enough about you to meet your needs?"

GOD IS HELPER

Many years ago, I wrote a tract entitled "Rescue". It tells of a man sinking in a deep pit and crying, "Help me! Help me!" An interesting procession of would-be rescuers stops and tells the sinking man how to get out. One says, "lift yourself by your own bootstraps!" He doesn't even provide the bootstraps. Another said, "That's not mud down there. Get mud out of your mind, and you'll be free." Another makes a speech, "When you come to the end of your rope, tie a knot and hang on" And he throws down a rope, both ends. A committee, after a long meeting, decides to throw down a new suit, books to read, a flashlight and a transistor radio to the man at the bottom of the pit. They all represent false philosophies and religions such as humanitarianism, humanism, intellectualism, agnosticism, hedonism and many others. At the end of the drama, Jesus comes by, stops, hears the cries and leaps down into the pit. He lifts the man up so his feet are on solid ground. Then He calls from the bottom of the pit, "Go and sin no more; you are free," as He, the Lord of Glory, the Creator of the ends of the earth sinks in the mire and dies.

Indeed, God is our **Helper**, the one who responds to our cries for help.

"*Behold, **God is my helper**;*
the Lord is the upholder of my life."
PSALM 54:4

*"He drew me up from the desolate pit,
out of the miry bog, and set my feet upon a rock,
making my steps secure."*
PSALM 40:2

On a recent Sunday evening, I was in the Shakopee Prison for Women for the closing service of a three-day Charis Prison Ministry weekend. My daughter, Anne, and her husband, Paul, were part of a team of forty persons who had trained for six months for this mission. They were assisted by twenty "insiders" who had gone through the program. For three days, from 8:00 in the morning to 9:00 at night, forty-two women in the prison were taught the way of new life and hope in Christ. They were affirmed, loved and listened to; they were feted at a banquet as honored guests. On Sunday night they marched into the prison gym to a standing ovation. Their faces were radiant. Their testimonies of Jesus' love that had been revealed to them told of their transformed lives. Words cannot describe their moving testimonies. Some had committed murder. Now they were paying society's price, but they knew that they were saved and free because Jesus was killed on a cross for them. As I heard these women, I thought that only they and God could know the unspeakable lives of suffering they had lived, and for many, the abuse endured before landing in prison. What a memorable night, a night of wonders and miracles! I should add that the team members were very much aware that it would be difficult for the forty-two guests of honor to descend from this mountaintop experience to the deep, dark valley of reality, away from home, children and freedom. The team members, in order to participate in a Charis weekend, pledged themselves to one year of monthly visits back to the prison, there to shepherd, encourage, affirm and support these new children in the Kingdom.

Indeed, our Lord is a very present help to persons deeply and severely impaired in body, mind and spirit. They are in places of defeat and failure. In every place, the Lord is there to help people who are willing to look and listen to this great God and Friend and Saviour.

On Easter Sunday at a family gathering, we called my grand-daughter who was studying at Uppsala University in Sweden. When it was my turn to speak with her, I started by saying, "Katie, have you heard the good news? The great news?" Perhaps Katie was wondering at this point what the good news might be, "Are you coming to visit me? Did a cousin become engaged?" But I kept repeating, "Katie, I want to tell you about the good news. Katie, the risen Saviour is in Stockholm and by your side!" Indeed, Katie knew full well and testified to the fact that God, in the person of Jesus, was very present with her to give her all the help she needed.

GOD IS HOLY

At my age of 91 I suppose I am more vulnerable to the temptation of looking back and glorying in the past. I hope that I look back just long enough to be aware of the marvelous things that God has done as we read of them in Psalm 98:1:

*"O sing to the Lord a new song, for he has done marvelous things! His right hand and his **holy** arm have gotten him victory."*

*"Extol the Lord our God, and worship at his holy mountain; for the Lord our God is **holy**!"*
PSALM 99:9

I do believe, however, that my memories of the past help keep me going at this time in my life journey. For example, I recall as a child coming into the sanctuary on a Sunday morning and hearing the organ prelude followed by a song of praise and adoration. Then at the beginning of the liturgical service I would hear these words, "Holy, Holy, Holy is the Lord of Hosts. The whole earth is full of His glory. The Lord is in His Holy Temple. His throne is in heaven. The Lord is nigh unto them who are of an humble and contrite spirit. He hears the supplications of the penitent and inclines to their prayers. Let us therefore draw near with confidence to His throne of grace and confess our sins." There I found myself in the presence of a holy, awe-inspiring God!

Once again I turn to my wife Marta for help in the **God is holy** picture. This poem, taken from her book, *From Grey to Gold*, is entitled "A Grandmother's Gift".

"At deepest dusk
my grandmother took me on her lap.

She pointed to the black velvet of night outside the window,
and her hand outlined the vastness of the unknown,
and she said, 'God'.

From that moment on, I knew that
God was not a grandfather figure
who carried on his back a Santa Claus bag of
sweet surprises.

He is, rather, the one to whom belongs
the words, ineffable, unsearchable,
and above all,
holy.

And so it was that my grandmother took my hand
And together we touched
the heartbeat of the universe,
the secret place of the Most High.
Forever after,
God was holy."

G O D   I S   L O V E

"So we know and believe the love God has for us.
***God is love**, and he who abides in love abides in God,*
and God abides in him."
I JOHN 4:16

I believe it is necessary to dwell at some length and in detail on this affirmation, **God is love**. Indeed, we need to learn the meaning of love. In the television wasteland of today, in the lust-laden lyrics and in the R and X-rated movies, we see the prostitution of love and the degrading of human life.

Volumes of books are written about love, love that is counterfeit, shallow and immature, books about lust masquerading as love. The sexual revolution, which offers freedom from all moral restraints, has created the most tied-up generation in history. The results are broken homes and lives, epidemics of sexual disease and the demeaning of the human body and spirit.

Where shall we go to learn the meaning of true love? We were created to love and to be loved. Therefore, we turn to our Creator who is the source of true love. In fact, He **is** love as we read in I John 4:7-11:

> "*Beloved, let us love one another; for love is of God, and he who loves is born of God and knows God. He who does not love does not know God; for* **God is love.** *In this the love of God was manifested toward us, that God has sent His only Son into the world, so that we might live through Him. In this is love, not that we loved God but that He loved us and sent His Son to be the expiation for our sins. Beloved, if God so loved us, we also ought to love one another.*"

I recall an old story of a bride whose first attempt to cook dinner for her husband was a catastrophe. (This story is not about brides that cannot cook. Many brides are excellent cooks. It is a story about love.) The meat was tough, the salad came in liquid form and the potatoes were soggy. However, the husband ate heartily and cheerfully with no complaint. After the meal he got up and hugged and kissed his wife passionately. When she could recover, she said, "I just don't understand this. I know that I did an awful job with this dinner and yet you hugged me." Her husband explained, "Today you prepared a meal such as a bride would prepare, so I wanted to treat you as a bride."

God loves us struggling sinners in the midst of our failures and wasted opportunities. He loves us into loving Him and into loving others.

Here are some thoughts on eros and agape love by Anders Mygren, a Swedish theologian: "Eros is acquisitive desire and longing. Agape is sacrificial giving. Eros is an upward movement.

Agape comes down. Eros is man's way to God. Agape is God's way to man. Eros is man's effort. . .Agape is God's grace. . .Eros is primarily man's love —God is the object of Eros. . .Eros recognizes value in its object and loves it. Agape loves and creates value in its object."

God is love! How can we know this? By reading John 3:16:

> *"For God so loved the world that he gave his only Son,*
> *that whoever believes in him should not perish*
> *but have eternal life."*

Dr. E. Stanley Jones reminds us that agape love takes a dangerous risk. Perhaps this is why so many persons, unwilling to accept "suffering love", embrace human love instead of God's love. Dr. Jones writes in his book, *A Song of Ascents*, as follows:

> "I have often wondered why God created man and made him free. That was a dangerous thing to do. Suppose man would go wrong and abuse that freedom; then God would have to stand alongside that will as love. He couldn't coerce him, for a coerced goodness is not goodness at all. But to stand alongside sin in the loved one means that God would suffer, for it is the nature of love to insinuate itself into the sins and sorrows of the loved one and make them its own. If love stays out, it is not love. If it gets in, it bleeds. All love has the doom of bleeding upon it as long as there is sin in the loved one. Then why did God take that risk?
>
> "Why do parents take that risk? It is a dangerous thing to bring a child into the world. Suppose that child goes wrong. It will break its own heart and the hearts of the parents. Then why do parents create? Because love wants an object of love upon whom it can lavish that love and be loved in return. . . Being love, he (God) could not sit and contemplate his perfections forever. He would want to impart that love, would want creatures upon whom he could lavish his love and be loved in return. But it would be on the understanding that if that creation of his goes wrong it would fall on God. For

love would reach out and make the sin its own. So the moment man sinned there would be an unseen cross upon the heart of God. That is the meaning of this passage: the 'Lamb slain from the foundation of the world.' From the foundation of the world—I thought it was two thousand years ago? No, the unseen cross would be on the heart of God 'from the foundation of the world', the moment man sinned. But how would we know that? God is an unseen Spirit. How would we know there is an unseen cross upon the heart of God? We couldn't unless he should lift up an outer cross in history to let us see through that outer cross, the unseen cross on the heart of God. The outer cross with its self-giving love lights up the nature of God as self-giving love. Self-giving love is at the center of the universe—the 'Lamb who is at the heart of the throne'. That is the highest, absolutely the highest, revelation about God and the nature of reality that has ever been given or can be given."

Indeed, we see the meaning of love at the cross.

> *"By this we know love, that he laid down his life for us;*
> *and we ought to lay down our lives for the brethren."*
> I JOHN 3:16

Here is breathtaking news. God offers His self-giving love, the highest gift that any human being could ever receive, to every believer in Him and in His Son Jesus Christ. My mind cannot comprehend the wonder and miracle of it all. God offers His love to us, His children, to share with others. Thus it becomes the highest and most precious gift we can give to anyone. Indeed, we are told in God's Word that the greatest commandment of all is to love our God above all things and our neighbor as ourselves.

> *"And one of them, a lawyer, asked him a question, to test*
> *him. 'Teacher, which is the great commandment in the*
> *law?' And he said to him, 'You shall love the Lord your God*
> *with all your heart, and with all your soul, and with all*

*your mind. This is the great and first commandment. And
a second is like it. You shall love your neighbor as yourself.
On these two commandments depend all the law and the
prophets.'"*
MATTHEW 22:35-40

Each day I pray for those who are living in poverty and especially for those who are dying from hunger. I am aware that my
prayers are no substitute for obedience. One of the most significant charitable gifts that anyone can give is a gift for the hungry
of the world. But there is a greater tragedy than starving without
food. I call it poverty of love. There is no greater impoverishment than to live and die without love. In the context of this
chapter, it is surely clear that we are speaking of agape love. This
is indeed God's love as revealed in Jesus Christ.

Now let us pose a troubling question. Why is it that many in
the Christian Church and in Christian institutions choose to
tone down expressions of this supreme gift of our God? I read
many statements of faith that talk about God and neighbor and
reaching out to others and doing good. But the highest expression of being good neighbors and a caring community is found
only in God's love as revealed in Jesus Christ. We hear much talk
about inclusive ministry. There is nothing more inclusive than
the love of God. We recall the heart of the gospel, **"God so loved
the world. . ."** This means a world of sinners like us, sinners from
every nation and tribe and people and culture and life style.
How can we be more inclusive than to heed the words of Jesus
in Matthew 11:28:

> *"Come to me, all who labor and are heavy laden,
> and I will give you rest."*

How can we be more inclusive than to follow the example of
Jesus who said:

> *"The Spirit of the Lord is upon me, because he has
> anointed me to preach good news to the poor. He has sent
> me to proclaim release to the captives and recovering of*

sight to the blind, to set at liberty those who are oppressed,
to proclaim the acceptable year of the Lord."
LUKE 4:18, 19

We can learn much from Gandhi, a Hindu, and an apostle of non-violence and peace. In a conversation taken from his book, *The Christ of the Indian Road*, Stanley Jones, a good friend of Gandhi, asked him this question , "Could you tell me what you think we as Christians should do to make Christianity more naturalized in India...something which contributes power to India's uplift and redemption?" He immediately replied, "I would suggest four things: First, that all you Christians, missionaries and all, must begin to live more like Jesus Christ. Second, that you practice your religion without adulterating it, or toning it down. Third, that you emphasize love and make it your working force, for love is central to Christianity. Fourth, that you study the non-Christian religions more sympathetically to find the good in them, to have a more sympathetic approach to the people."

With these words of Gandhi in mind, should we not hang our heads in shame as betrayers of our Lord and Saviour when we hesitate to speak of Him and His love for fear that we might offend those of other religions or of no religion?

I sat with Stanley Jones at a Rotary meeting in a city many years ago. In that gathering there were Jews, Christians, Universalists, believers and non-believers. He spoke on the verses found in Ephesians 2:14,15:

"For he is our peace, who has made us both one,
and has broken down the dividing wall of hostility,
by abolishing in his flesh the law of commandments and
ordinances, that he might create in himself one new man
in place of the two, so making peace."

At the end of his message, he received a rousing round of applause.

At another gathering of leaders in a city, he gave his usual Christ-centered, Word-centered and practical life-centered message. When he sat down, he turned to the Jewish Rabbi and said, "Rabbi, was I too Christian for you?" The Rabbi replied, "No

86

indeed, the more Christian you are the better you will treat us and all people."

Someone may ask, "Well, if God is so loving, how can He condemn some people to eternal punishment in the next life?" At this point I think Stanley Jones can help us again. I quote from his book, *The Unshakable Kingdom and the Unchanging Person.*

"God redeems, recreates, and rules the world from a cross of self-giving love. The ultimate is good will toward everybody, everywhere even toward those who are in revolt against that good will.

"But it is not a grandfatherly good will which says: 'It's all right with me no matter what you do.' A vast moral indifference is not at the center. God, our Father, as I've said before, has two hands—the hand of grace, and the hand of judgment. If you won't take grace from the hand of grace, you will have to take it from the hand of judgment. The judgment is that you decay by the very revolt, and if the revolt is persisted in, you perish. But when the last flickering light goes out there would be a teardrop on the cheek of grace and the requiem words on the lips of grace, 'But ye would not.' Love and the Law combine at the center—love that redeems and law that restrains, restrains from self-destruction. Both are love. He has to uphold the universe by law and has to redeem man and the universe by love. But they are two sides of one fact. Love, self-giving love, is at the heart of the throne."

Let me close this chapter with a story from the same book:

"A college president was about to introduce me to his student body when he asked me if I remembered writing a letter twenty years ago to a young pastor who felt inferior because his father had disgraced the family name. I not only remembered, but I remembered my reply: 'In the genealogy of Jesus was this item: 'Solomon was born of David by Uriah's wife.' Did that ugly patch in his ancestral past break Jesus or cloud him? No, for he was more conscious of his heredity from his Father God, the heredity upward canceled the heredity backward. You can have a blood transfusion from the Son of God that will cancel the tainted blood of ancestors. You can be born from above and not be born back there.' 'Yes,' he said, 'I saw it and took it and all my inferiorities dropped away and that's why I am a college president.'"

So much more could be said about **God is Love**. The subject is inexhaustible. Perhaps the words of a song, "O Love That Will Not Let Me Go", will help us in a moment of reconsecration and rededication of our lives to our Lord and Saviour.

"O Love that wilt not let me go,
  I rest my weary soul in Thee;
  I give Thee back the life I owe,
  That in Thine ocean depths its flow
  May richer, fuller be."

Because **God is** in Jesus, I am indeed **OKAY** in Him!

OKAYED FOR SERVICE
IN CHURCH AND WORLD

CHAPTER SEVEN

In studying the nature and mission of the Church, I have often thought that the Church exists primarily for those outside its fellowship. It means that God's army is trained within the walls in order to engage in costly discipleship in the world. Indeed, what shall it profit the Church if she perfects her techniques and has no redemptive message for lost and hurting persons in the world? Martin Luther said, "Believing in Christ as your neighbor means being Christ to your neighbor."

"Go therefore and make disciples of all nations,
baptizing them in the name of the Father
and of the Son and of the Holy Spirit,
teaching them to observe all that I have commanded you;
and lo, I am with you always, to the close of the age."
MATTHEW 28:19,20

OKAYED FOR SERVICE IN CHURCH AND WORLD

I n the Matthew passage, the "lo I am with you" is for those who go in obedience to our Lord's command. But what about those who cannot go and make disciples? His call is also **to be** and **to belong**. It is not only what we do but also who we are and whose we are. We are called to reflect His presence. Martin Luther said that we are to be called "little Christ's". Wonder of Wonders! Indeed, we are called to practice His Presence and **to be** His Presence

Recently, I received a letter from a widow who told me that her husband had been killed in an auto accident. He had been serving as a medical missionary in Mexico for many years. He was on his way to take care of desperately ill persons in a clinic. I met this doctor when he was a member of the youth group in my first parish in the 1940's. In my letter to his wife, I reminded her that the thousands of people to whom he had ministered in both body and spirit knew who he was. Perhaps as they waited in the clinic, they would look up and say, "Here comes the healer. Here comes our doctor-friend." But it would be more accurate to say, "Here comes the Jesus man." It may be that some would regard this as spiritual arrogance. They might be the ones who never want to be called saints inasmuch as they forget that a saint is a rescued sinner.

We are called not only to practice the presence of God, but also to practice **His inner presence.**

In Colossians 1:27 we read these words:

> *"To them God chose to make known how great among the Gentiles are the riches of the glory of this mystery, which is Christ in you, the hope of glory."*

Christ in you! Wonder of Wonders! And more. It is the miracle that happened at Pentecost.

Let us review for a moment. Christmas is the festival of **God**

with us. It's the miracle of Incarnation. We read these words in Matthew 1:23:

> *"Behold, a virgin shall conceive and bear a son, and his name shall be called Emmanuel (which means, **God with us**)."*

The Bible unfolds for us an even greater miracle, **God for us**. We read of this in I Timothy 2:5,6:

> *"For there is one God, and there is one mediator between God and men, the man Christ Jesus, who gave himself as a ransom for all, the testimony to which was borne at the proper time."*

I believe that the greatest miracle of all happened at Pentecost. This is the miracle of **God in us**.

> *"Do you not know that you are God's temple and that God's Spirit dwells in you?"*
> I CORINTHIANS 3:16

> *"When the day of Pentecost had come, they were all together in one place. And suddenly a sound came from heaven like the rush of a mighty wind, and it filled all the house where they were sitting. And there appeared to them tongues as of fire, distributed and resting on each one of them. And they were all filled with the Holy Spirit and began to speak in other tongues, as the Spirit gave them utterance."*
> ACTS 2:1-4

Now let us come back to these words from Colossians 1:27: *"Christ in you, the hope of glory."* This reminds us of Martin Luther who taught that believers are called to be "little Christs". It also reminds us of something that Dietrich Bonhoeffer said. He was one of the great theologians of our generation or any other. We quote, "Christ became our brother in order to help us; now, through Him, our brother becomes for us a 'Christ' with all the authority of this commission. Our brother stands before us as a symbol of the truth and grace of God."

It follows that if Jesus Christ lives within us, wherever we go He goes. We are called to witness for Him, not only with words but most frequently by our "Christ-presence". To be called Christian should mean that we are called to be Christ-like.

A popular prayer before eating is, "Come Lord Jesus, be our guest. Let this food to us be blessed." But there will be no divine guest at our table if He is not a resident (and president!) in our hearts.

Another version of this prayer was given by the grandson of Hilvie Ostrow. Matthew, age seven, was troubled by the original version. He said, "We are God's guests. He's the one who gives us our food." Thus the new version was born: "Come, Lord Jesus, we are your guests. Let this food to us be blessed."

As I visit many severely impaired persons in the Augustana Health Care Center, I find some who cannot communicate with words. Some may not even recognize me. Some experience severe pain in the body. Many are in wheelchairs, and some are confined to their bed. But as we pray together, as I see many of them smile and as I hear them singing or repeating words of familiar songs or scriptures with me, I sense indeed that I am having a visit with Jesus.

OKAYED BY OUR CREATOR

Today are we especially vulnerable and indeed falling for the temptation that occurred at the dawn of Biblical history in the Garden of Eden? Satan planted doubt in the heart of Eve in the garden. In Genesis 3:1, we have this question, *"Did God say, 'You shall not eat of any tree of the garden?"* She informed him that God had said if they eat of the fruit of the tree which is in the midst of the garden or even touch it, they would die. Then we read in Genesis 3:4,5 these words of Satan, *"You will not die. For God knows that when you eat of it your eyes will be opened, and you will be like God, knowing good and evil."*

You will be like God! And when they believed the tempter rather than the word of God, their Creator, and when they aspired to be equal with God, they fell and great was the fall of the whole world with them. The ploughshare was drawn over paradise. The beautiful garden was turned into a shambles. The heavenly pair was expelled into the outer darkness. Ever since, in our fallen human nature, we have been tempted to "play God". So we come back to the question, "Who really is in charge of the okaying process?" Jesus said in John 15:16:

> *"You did not choose me, but I chose you and appointed*
> *you that you should go and bear fruit and that your fruit*
> *should abide; so that whatever you ask the Father*
> *in my name, he may give it to you."*

OKAYED TO BE THE CHURCH IN THE WORLD

Many years ago, I read the following lines in a parish paper in answer to the question, "What is my mission as the Church in the world?"

Not just to write a check,
  But to offer my life.
Not just to attend church,
  But to be the Church in the world.
Not just to serve the Church,
  But to serve my neighbor in need.
Not to preserve an institution
  But to love all men.
Not to keep people active,
  But to help them to be faithful.
Not to hold services,
  But to offer the grace of God.

The Church in the world. What does this mean? We could think of all inhabitants of the world. One dictionary describes "world' in terms of mortal existence in distinction from spiritual life. In this chapter, we think of the world, the whole earth, as **so loved** by our Creator that He gave His only Son to suffer and die to redeem his fallen world from the power of sin and death.

93

I like the view of the world of E. Stanley Jones. In his book, *A Song of Ascents*, he writes:

> "Jesus cleansed the idea of suffering from a sign of God's wrath, and made it into an opportunity to manifest His love and grace. Jesus cleansed the material earth from being an evil thing subject to doom and decay, and made it into the scene of the coming kingdom of God on earth. He cleansed the idea of the world condemned to the idea of the world as His unfinished creation. He cleansed the idea of women as subordinate and inferior to man to a place of equality and partnership. 'Thy kingdom come. . .on earth'—the earth is to be the subject and scene of redemption. It has a future. It is to be redeemed by the blood of the Son of God—His blood stains have rendered sacred forever the soil of the world."

I like to think of the Church as the people of God, **GATHERED — EQUIPPED — SCATTERED**. They gather at the cross. They are equipped there by the Holy Spirit. But we do not see the true Church of God until we see His people scattered in the world. There we are to be engaged in our Lord's ministry of healing and reconciliation. We sorely need this perspective of the Church. Too many think of the Church, as Elton Trueblood reminds us, "as people streaming to a shrine, or as making up an audience for a speaker".

In speaking of the Church in the world, perhaps we should think of our mission in terms of salt, light and leaven:

> *"You are the salt of the earth; but if salt has lost its taste, how shall its saltness be restored?"*
> MATTHEW 5:13A

> *"You are the light of the world. A city set on a hill cannot be hid."*
> MATTHEW 5:14

> *"Let us, therefore, celebrate the festival, not with the old leaven, the leaven of malice and evil,*

but with the unleavened bread of sincerity and truth."
I Corinthians 6:7

These Biblical views of the world and our place in it as His reborn creation, increase my EQ (Excitement Quotient) and my IQ (Involvement Quotient). This view of the world makes me an incurable optimist about God's world, even at my age of 91 years!

We need to ask the question, "What in the world is God doing?" And also, "What are we doing in God's world?"

Our concept of the Church in the world helps define the Church's mission in the world. For example, 35 years ago we started the Crossroad outreach ministry at Augustana Lutheran Church in Minneapolis, Minnesota. We built upon 100 years of Bible-centered, Christ-centered and Spirit-filled Word and Sacrament Ministry. Here we had the incentive and power for reaching across the street, across the city, nation and world to meet physical and spiritual needs of members of our "parish beyond the walls of the church". We became known as the place for weekly parking lot dinners, outdoor services of worship and witness, summer Crossroad School, mentoring, the Highway Camp for children and youth, Family of God tours for adults, dozens of interest groups (from hygiene to auto mechanics to cooking), food shelves that never ran out of food, financial help, job counseling, an AA group, Christian film and drama center and many others.

However, we were not known primarily as an "activity place". We became known by those outside the church as the Crossroad Church. Being interpreted, this means, "The way of the Cross—the way of the self-giving love of Jesus, and the way of sharing His love with others."

In studying the nature and mission of the Church, I have often thought that the Church exists primarily for those outside its fellowship. It means that God's army is trained within the walls in order to engage in costly discipleship in the world. Indeed, what shall it profit the Church if she perfects her techniques and has no redemptive message for lost and hurting persons in the world? Martin Luther said, "Believing in Christ as your neighbor means being a Christ to your neighbor."

95

*"By this we know love, that he laid down his life for us;
and we ought to lay down our lives for the brethren."*
I JOHN 3:16

In 1974, one of the Crossroad staff members painted a picture. In it three persons remain on the parking lot following Crossroad activities involving hundreds of persons on stage and in the audience. Jesus is telling two little children that He loves them and that they belong to Him. The angels of God stand guard to protect this sacred moment. And it happens under the cross.

Are we okay, ready to be the Church in the world? I need to pray the prayer of John Baillie in his book, *A Diary of Private Prayer,* "From unwillingness to learn and unreadiness to serve, O God, set me free."

To be okayed for service in the world means that we are willing to let God prepare us for servanthood.

*"For what we preach is not ourselves, but Jesus Christ as
Lord, with ourselves as your servants for Jesus' sake."*
II CORINTHIANS 4:5

I read of a deacon in an inner-city church who objected to his church's ministry to poor, homeless and hungry persons. He was shocked when his pastor told him who he really was. He said, "You are a deacon. This word means 'dia'—through and 'konos'—dust, a reference to the figure of a camel driver leading a camel through the dust while someone else rides on the beast of burden."

Some years ago, I preached a sermon on the theme, "There's Something Missing in Religion." I presented five pictures of barren religion: proselytism without conversion, piety without charity, authority without integrity, display without devotion, and activity without humility. The text was Matthew 23:1-12.

True humility is rooted in reverence for God and for persons. To be truly great means to be humble enough to be a servant. Here is a question I ask of myself, "Am I humble enough to be amazed at the divine miracle of being called and chosen and okayed to serve the Creator and Lord of Glory in His redemptive work in the world?"

OKAYED FOR PERSON-TO-PERSON SERVICE

The parking lot picture reminds us of the words of Jesus in Matthew 25:40:

> *"Truly, I say to you, as you did it to one of the least*
> *of these my brethren, you did it to me."*

Every child, youth and adult, in whatever condition or circumstance they come, are God's gift to His Church.

I recall this reminder to Sunday School teachers, "O teacher in the Sunday School don't say, 'I've had enough.' That worst boy in your class may be a diamond in the rough."

Many years ago, I participated in the follow-through program of the Billy Graham New York Crusade. I recall how we knocked on doors of those who had signed commitment cards in the city. Telephone calls, letters and e-mail surely can bring many into the fellowship of the Church. However, there is no substitute for the personal touch.

In 1971, I served on the Central Planning Committee for the Billy Graham Crusade in St. Paul, Minnesota. At the close of the crusade, I received a list of the names of persons who had responded to the altar call. As a parish pastor, I was expected to be sure that each one on the list would be contacted personally. These persons had either expressed interest in our Augustana Church or lived in our community. If we were not interested in making these follow-up visits, we were asked to return the names to the committee so others could make the calls.

The ministry of Jesus surely highlights the importance of service to individuals in need. How true it is that *"God so loved the world"*—the whole wide world and every person in it. But there is also a "whosoever" in that John 3:16 verse. As we affirm John 3:16, I think that it would be beneficial for us at intervals to substitute our name for the word "world". Indeed, God so loved William that he gave his only Son.

97

OKAYED FOR PARADISE REGAINED

I am writing this chapter on May 29, 2001, which is being observed as Memorial Day. This afternoon we visited the grave of my life partner, Marta, who went home to be forever with her Lord on Thanksgiving Day, 1996. In the cemetery we heard the angel speaking to the women who came on that first Easter morning to the tomb of Jesus. The angel stood at the empty tomb and spoke to the trembling women as recorded in Mark 16:6,7:

> *"And he said to them, 'Do not be amazed; you seek*
> *Jesus of Nazareth, who was crucified. He has risen, he is*
> *not here; see the place where they laid him. But go,*
> *tell his disciples and Peter that he is going before you to*
> *Galilee; there you will see him, as he told you.'"*

We rejoiced that Marta was not in that grave. She had gone before us into the heavenly Galilee where we would be sure to meet her some day. We also remembered the words of Revelation 14:13:

> *"And I heard a voice from heaven saying, 'Write this:*
> *Blessed are the dead who die in the Lord henceforth.'*
> *'Blessed indeed,' says the Spirit, 'that they may rest from*
> *their labors, for their deeds follow them!'"*

Surely, their deeds follow them. Marta had been okayed for beautiful, fruitful service during her lifetime. We read one of her poems from her book, *Seen and Unseen*. The title is "A Falling Leaf".

> "Watch a copper-colored leaf
> spiral down to the ground.
>
> As it falls, it foretells chill and
> the sharp edge of wind.
>
> It signifies separation.

But more —
As it falls,
it whispers to our consciousness,
'God.'

For God is master of the cycles of life and death.

The leaf falls and dies.
At the same time,
it nurtures the earth, and it becomes
part of the mystery
of renewed life.

In death, then, is the promise of new life.

Therefore, fear not.
Fret not.
Rest in God's design."

Now let me share something that some readers will regard as too sentimental or emotional, but it was very real to me. I heard Marta say, "God commissioned us to serve together. He gave us the greatest honor that could come to us, namely to be okayed for a lifetime of service for Him and for others. I am now in my Saviour's nearer presence, being prepared for service in my brand new body in my Father's house. You are still chosen for service down there. Carry on! There is more for you to do before you come Home."

This reverie reminds me that to be okayed for Kingdom service for our Lord in this world is preparation for the perfect service He will enable us to give in our eternal Home. C. S. Lewis in his book, *Mere Christianity*, writes:

"A continual looking forward to the eternal world is not (as some modern people think) a form of escapism or wishful thinking, but one of the things a Christian is meant to do. It does not mean that we are to leave the present world as it is. If you read history you will find that the Christians who did most for the present world were just those who thought most of the next. The Apostles themselves, who set on foot the conversion of the Roman Empire, the great men who built up the

Middle Ages, the English Evangelicals who abolished the Slave Trade, all left their mark on Earth precisely because their minds were occupied with Heaven. It is since Christians have largely ceased to think of the other world that they have become so ineffective in this. Aim at Heaven and you will get earth thrown in; aim at earth and you will get neither."

On this Memorial Day, buglers all over our country in thousands of cemeteries have played the familiar song, "Taps". Most versions of the origin of this song give credit to General Dan Butterfield and his bugler, Olivier Norton. It was written in 1862 to commemorate the loss of nearly 11,000 lives, soldiers from both sides, who fell in the Civil War.

However, there is another version with the title, "Urban Legend". It all supposedly began in 1862 during the Civil War, when Union Army Captain Robert Ellicombe was with his men near Harrison's Landing in Virginia. The Confederate Army was on the other side of the narrow strip of land. During the night, Captain Ellicombe heard the moan of a soldier who lay severely wounded on the field. Not knowing if it was a Union or Confederate soldier, the Captain decided to risk his life and bring the stricken man back for medical attention. Crawling on his stomach through the gunfire, the Captain reached the stricken soldier and began pulling him toward his encampment. When the Captain finally reached his own lines, he discovered it was actually a Confederate soldier, but the soldier was dead. The Captain lit a lantern. Suddenly he caught his breath and went numb with shock. In the dim light, he saw the face of the soldier. It was his own son. The boy had been studying music in the South when the war broke out. Without telling his father, he had enlisted in the Confederate Army. The following morning, heartbroken, the father asked permission of his superiors to give his son a full military burial despite his enemy status. His request was partially granted. The Captain had asked if he could have a group of Army band members play a funeral dirge for his son at the funeral. The request was turned down since the soldier was a Confederate. Out of respect for the father, they did say they could give him one musician.

The Captain chose a bugler. He asked the bugler to play a series of musical notes he had found on a piece of paper in the pocket of his dead son's uniform. This wish was granted. The haunting melody we now know as "Taps" was born.

> "Day is done,
>   Gone the sun,
>   From the lake,
>   From the hill,
>   From the sky.
>   All is well,
>   Safely rest,
>   God is nigh."

Having come to terms with our Lord's **Divine IF**, and having been okayed for service in this world and in heaven forever, may we hear, not taps, but the footsteps of our Saviour coming to take us into continuing service in our eternal Home.

Our Lord reminds us to "carry on" in a reassuring promise in I Chronicles 28:20:

> *"Be strong and of good courage, and do it.*
> *Fear not, be not dismayed; for the Lord God,*
> *even my God, is with you. He will not fail you or*
> *forsake you, until all the work for the service*
> *of the house of the Lord is finished."*

This is a divine word, not only for King Solomon and the building of the temple, but surely also for us today.

This final word. Don't listen for taps. Listen for this Word from Psalm 85:9:

> *"Surely his salvation is nigh them that fear him;*
> *that glory may dwell in our land."* (KJV)

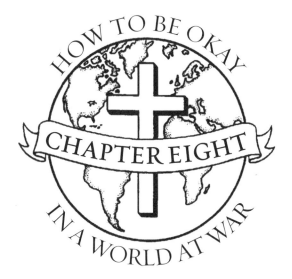

HOW TO BE OKAY
CHAPTER EIGHT
IN A WORLD AT WAR

At this writing, wars are being waged in Afghanistan, the Middle East and other places in our world. My country is involved in a war against terrorism. How can anyone possibly be Okay in such a world? Can any good come out of terrible disasters?

"And now, Lord, look upon their threats,
and grant to thy servants to speak thy word with all
boldness, while thou stretchest out thy hand to heal,
and signs and wonders are performed through
the name of thy holy servant, Jesus."
ACTS 4:29-30

HOW TO BE OKAY IN
A WORLD AT WAR

This chapter was not planned for my book, but it had to be written and included.

But how can we possibly relate the "Day of Infamy" (September 11, 2001) to the title and message of this book? Hopefully, we will find the answer, not in my words but in our Lord's divine Word.

"If you continue in my word, you are truly my disciples,
and you will know the truth, and the truth
will make you free."
JOHN 8:31,32

Free to hope! Free to be okay in a world torn by terrorism, tragedy and war.

I wrote this part of the chapter on the evening of September 11. That day, I believe, will go down as one of the most memorable, tragic and shocking days in American history. On that day our nation came under enemy attack. Two hijacked planes hit the Twin Towers of the World Trade Center in New York City, causing them to collapse in a sea of smoke and rubble. Nearly three thousand persons lost their lives, their graveyard a place of smoldering steel. The pain and horror of this trajedy are beyond human comprehension.

A third hijacked plane hit the Pentagon in Washington, DC, causing enormous damage and many casualties. A fourth hijacked plane, which many believe was headed for the White House in Washington, DC, crashed near Pittsburgh. Two hundred and sixty-six persons perished in four plane crashes.

The day was described as "a Day of Infamy" in recollection of the words of Franklin Delano Roosevelt following the attack by Japan on Pearl Harbor in 1941. Indeed, it was a national tragedy of enormous magnitude.

Another thought crowds into my mind already filled with heaviness and shock. We will now be involved in another world war as a result of this heinous and cowardly attack upon our nation. I have a broad perspective of war and the use of military might during my 91 years of life. History will reveal that military might is often used to fulfill a short term and immediate objective, namely, to bring the terrorists to judgment. This is as necessary in a fallen world as it is to have a police force in a city, protecting its citizens from criminal assault. However, history will also reveal that the long-term objectives of peace, justice and freedom for all people are seldom fulfilled by war and bombs that inevitably kill both innocent and guilty persons. For example, World War I did not save the world for democracy. Indeed, it helped create a climate for Nazism and Fascism. World War II, though it conquered these enemies, was followed by the rise of Communism and the Cold War. The Vietnam War did not liberate South Vietnam from the tyranny of Communism. The war of Desert Storm did not do away with the menace of a rogue country and its tyrannical dictator.

Of course, our military might is reassuring in a world where many enemies want more than anything else to destroy our nation. But I have to ask for the gift of skepticism when I hear a crescendo of voices indicating that war is the answer. I want to test them in the crucible of history's lessons, common sense and above all, Eternal Truth!

I recall the words of an ancient king in the Bible. His name is King Jehoshaphat. God's chosen people, Israel, were being surrounded by an enemy coming to annihilate them. In II Chronicles 20:12b, the king said something that is very difficult for us proud Americans to say, "Lord, we do not know what to do." Then he added, "But our eyes are turned upon thee."

But now I ask, "How can anyone possibly be okay in a world like this at such a time as this? Can any good possibly come out of this indescribable disaster?" Indeed, we have pictures forever engraven on our minds that lift and inspire us. Can we ever forget the valiant and heroic efforts of the members of the New York City Fire Department, many of whom gave their lives in the rescue operation?

As a people we are coming together across racial, political, economic and social lines. We are coming together, not only to commiserate, to express horror and grief, anger and rage, sorrow and pain, but we are coming together as a nation to pray, to recall that we are "one nation, under God, indivisible". I have attended many prayer services. More than ever before, we are looking within ourselves and we are looking up to behold the God of justice, mercy and grace.

We are pressed to face the question again, "What do you believe?" But there's a more important question, "Whom do you trust?" or "In Whom do you believe?" Psalm 50:15 gives an answer:

*"I want you to trust me in your times of trouble,
so that I can rescue you and you can give me glory."*

The remainder of this chapter was written during the five weeks following the tragedy. My theme is, *"Praise God From Whom All Blessings Flow"*. This may sound strange in the context of recent events. I begin with an article, the origin of which I have not been able to trace.

"On Monday there were people fighting against praying
   in schools.
*On Tuesday you would have been hard pressed to find a
   school where someone was not praying.*

On Monday there were people who were trying
   to separate each other by race, sex, color and creed.
On Tuesday they were all holding hands.

On Monday we thought that we were secure.
On Tuesday we learned better.

On Monday we were talking about heroes
   as being athletes.
On Tuesday we relearned what hero meant.

On Monday people were fighting the Ten
   Commandments on government property.
*On Tuesday the same people said, 'God help us all' while
   thinking 'Thou shall not kill'.*

On Monday people argued with their kids about picking up their room.
On Tuesday the same people could not get home fast enough to hug their kids.

On Monday people picked up McDonalds for dinner.
On Tuesday they stayed home.

On Monday politicians argued about budget surpluses.
On Tuesday, grief stricken, they sang 'God Bless America'.

On Monday some children had solid families.
On Tuesday they were orphans."

I added one additional thought:

On Monday the advocates of moral relativism were vocal and self-assured.
On Tuesday they were talking about the reality of good and evil.

Now I shall try to answer the question, "How to be Okay in a World at War", with a series of "*IFS*".

IT'S OKAY TO BE ANGRY AT A TIME LIKE THIS, *IF.*

Uncontrolled anger can turn into a deadly spirit of rage and revenge which destroys lives, including the life of the enraged person. We need to follow the admonition of our Lord in His word:

> *"Be angry but do not sin;*
> *do not let the sun go down on your anger."*
> EPHESIANS 4:26

IT'S OKAY TO BE FRIGHTENED, *IF.*

Fear is a healthy instinct, given for our protection and survival. Fear can also be paralyzing. It can destroy initiative. Fear is okay if we will follow the example of an elderly woman in a ship at sea during a violent storm. She found her way to the bridge where the captain was at the helm. She said, "Captain, I'm frightened. I'm terrified. Do you think we will make it through this awful storm?" The captain shouted, "Lady, you listen to me. This is a leaky old boat and we may go down. The boilers are in bad shape and we may go up. But lady, whatever happens, we're going on!"

Fear is indeed okay **if** we keep our eyes upon the captain of our salvation and **if** we remember His word:

> *"Fear not, for I am with you, be not dismayed,*
> *for I am your God; I will strengthen you, I will help you,*
> *I will uphold you with my victorious right hand."*
> ISAIAH 41:10

IT'S OKAY TO CRY, *IF.*

Our tears of anger, self-pity, defeat, grief, pain and frustration can be transformed into tears of penitence, faith, hope, love, joy and peace. Tears can be used to give us clear vision of the divine and ultimate plan of our Lord. And someday all crying will cease.

> *"For the Lamb in the midst of the Throne will be their*
> *shepherd, and He will guide them to springs of living*
> *water; and God will wipe away every tear from their eyes."*
> REVELATION 7:17

IT'S OKAY TO ASK "WHY?", *IF.*

Indeed, our Lord understands when our human, stricken spirit cries, "Why? Why terrorists? Why so many victims of terrifying crimes and violence and accidents?" I believe the answer lies in Jesus' cry from His cross of torture:

> *"My God, my God,*
> *why hast thou forsaken me?"*
> MARK 15:34c

Why indeed? Jesus, our Saviour, died on the cross to conquer sin and death, evil and the devil. Then, on the Resurrection Morning, He arose from the dead to confirm that victory and to remind us that evil does not have the last word. The enemies of God can crucify His Son on Friday. But on Easter Sunday, we claim and proclaim His victory.

> *"O death, where is thy victory? O death, where is thy sting?*
> *The sting of death is sin, and the power of sin is the law.*
> *But thanks be to God, who gives us the victory*
> *through our Lord Jesus Christ."*
> I Corinthians 15:55-57

IT'S OKAY TO WALK IN DARKNESS, *IF.*

Someone said, "Don't criticize someone who is afraid of the dark. Try praying for the person who is afraid of the light." Light indeed magnifies darkness. Walking often in the dark, let us take courage in these reassuring words from our Lord."

> *"The people who walked in darkness have seen a great*
> *light; those who dwelt in a land of deep darkness,*
> *on them has light shined."*
> Isaiah 9:2

IT'S OKAY TO LAMENT AND GROAN AND BE HEAVY-HEARTED, *IF.*

Are we willing to move from lament to praise? The prophet, Jeremiah, reminds us of this crucial move.

> *"My soul continually thinks of it and is bowed down*
> *within me. But this I call to mind, and therefore I have hope:*
> *The steadfast love of the Lord never ceases, his mercies*
> *never come to an end; they are new every morning; great*
> *is thy faithfulness. 'The Lord is my portion,' says my soul,*
> *'therefore I will hope in him'."*
> Lamentations 3:20-24

How to be okay in a world at war? The answer: *Praise God From Whom All Blessings Flow.* So now we remind ourselves of seven blessings among countless others, blessings that our Lord is offering to us in the midst of calamity and war.

PRAISE GOD FOR A SONG IN THE NIGHT.

Praise Him for the sound of singing in front of the National Capital in Washington, DC as members of Congress sang, "God Bless America". Praise God for the sound of singing in the Washington Cathedral as our President and countless other leaders sang, "A Mighty Fortress Is Our God" and "Mine Eyes Have Seen The Glory Of The Coming Of The Lord". Praise God for the blessing of the song that never dies! I recall the words of Martin Luther in one of the stanzas of his hymn, "A Mighty Fortress Is Our God":

"Thy Word they still shall let remain,
   Nor any thanks have for it;
   He's by our side upon the plain.
   With His good gifts and Spirit.
   Take they, then, what they will,
   Life, goods, yea, all; and still,
   E'en when their worst is done,
   They yet have nothing won,
   The kingdom ours remaineth."

PRAISE GOD FOR THE GIFT OF INSIGHT

Instead of turning to God for help in this time of national crisis, some are turning against God, saying, "God did this to us."

We need to remember that God's sovereign will in creation was perfection for all of His children. He gave us the priceless gift of free will that makes us truly human. Beginning with Adam, the human race rebelled against His perfect plan for our lives. As we take a long look at the cross, we see the price He paid to redeem and rescue us. With our eyes on that cross, we will never ever again blame God for these disasters. Look again at the cross. There we see the cruel crown of thorns pressed upon the sacred brow of Jesus, torturing Him in order that you and I could wear the crown of glory that can never be taken away. See the dirty spittle of man's demonic hatred, running down the beautiful face of Jesus so that your face and mine might be radiant with an eternal hope. There at the cross, we hear the sickening thud of the hammer blows, nailing the spikes to Jesus' hands and feet in order that those hands could reach out to us saying, "I love you, I am with you, I will be with you always." Keep looking at the cross and see the robe of ridicule they put upon Jesus in order that He might give to us a robe of redemption to cover our filthy rags as we stand before a Holy God. We hear His cry from the cross, *"My God, my God, why have you forsaken me?"* This means that we will never need to walk alone in this dangerous world.

> *"Then he [Jesus] opened their minds to*
> *understand the scriptures."*
> LUKE 24:45

PRAISE GOD FOR THE GIFT OF TEARS.

I think that all of us have shed tears, many tears during these last few weeks. When I saw the pictures of those twin towers crumbling to the ground with thousands of helpless victims going to that graveyard, I cried out aloud and I shed tears. As we cry together, we are brought very close to one another. As I shed tears, I had to remember that my tears can never be as bitter and as heavy as the tears of those who have lost loved ones in this tragedy. But I can cry with them. I can cry with the families who are broken-hearted and devastated. Ah, yes, tears. They are a wonderful gift of our Lord. And there is a lot of health-inspiring therapy in the right kind of tears.

> *"For the Lamb in the midst of the Throne will be their*
> *shepherd, and He will guide them to springs of living*
> *water; and God will wipe away every tear from their eyes."*
> REVELATION 7:17

PRAISE GOD THAT THE PLACE OF TRAGEDY HAS BEEN TRANSFORMED INTO A PLACE OF PRAYER.

Our President set aside one day as a National Day of Prayer. Prayer not only changes things and changes our perspective, but it also changes us and keeps us looking up to see where our help comes from.

> *"Have no anxiety about anything, but in everything by prayer and supplication with thanksgiving let your requests be made known to God. And the peace of God, which passes all understanding, will keep your hearts and minds in Christ Jesus."*
> PHILIPPIANS 4:6-7

PRAISE GOD THAT HE IS SENDING A REASSURING MESSAGE TO HIS CHURCH.

> *"If my people who are called by my name humble themselves, and pray and seek my face, and turn from their wicked ways, then I will hear from heaven, and will forgive their sin and heal their land."*
> II CHRONICLES 7:14

Repentance! It is a key word. Without repentance, there will be no healing of the nation or nations. Whom is God calling to repent? He is calling us, *"His people who are called by His name,"* to turn from our wicked ways. This is the price of divine healing. God help us not to miss it!

PRAISE GOD FOR THE BLESSING OF FREEDOM OF WORSHIP.

It is indeed reassuring to live in a country where we have freedom of conscience and freedom of speech and freedom to worship our God. It is reassuring for me to know that I live in a country where separation of Church and State was never intended, by the founding fathers, to mean separation of the State from God, our Creator under whom our nation was founded and who sustains us. It was reassuring to hear President Bush quote Psalm 23:4 KJV:

> *"Yea, thou I walk through the valley of the shadow of death, I will fear no evil; for thou art with me. . ."*

PRAISE GOD FOR REMINDING US OF OUR MORTALITY.

We need to remember that death can strike any of us at any time, whatever our age or circumstance. Thousands of persons left home the morning of September 11, never dreaming they would not return.

In her book of narrative verse, *Seen and Unseen,* Marta wrote about verse 6 in Psalm 23:

> *"Surely goodness and mercy shall follow me all the days of my life, and I shall dwell in the house of the Lord forever."*

The title of her poem is "Surely":

"Surely goodness and mercy
shall follow me. . .

There was that word again—surely.

How can anyone say surely in a day of
tumultuous change?

Or had the Psalmist noted
that there is an absolute certainty
in the universe,
that God's law is unfailingly constant?

On the strength of its constancy,
persons can leave Earth and function in space.

The nurtured bud always opens into bloom.
Ice always forms at the freezing point.
Gravity never takes a vacation.

And so it is with God's moral law. . .
Repentance gives birth to joy.
Peace is a partner of trust.
Love opens doors closed by hate.

God's certainties are written into
the very heartbeat of life itself.

Yes, SURELY."

How to be okay in a world at war? Keep singing in the midst of the storm and the night and the suffering and the pain. Try His way!

PRAISE GOD FROM WHOM ALL BLESSINGS FLOW!

THANK YOU

To my children and grandchildren, Anne and J. Paul Carlson, Jon and Mari, Jeff and Katie; Bill and Karen Berg, Will and Ben; Paul Conrad, Steven and Karen (their mother, my daughter, Marcia, went to her eternal home in 1994). As I call the roll of family members, my song of praise rings out for these wonderful gifts from my Lord.

To my daughter, Anne, and my grandson, Jon, for the days and hours they spent in the editing process.

To Marta Berg, my life partner for 55 years. Her poems, her brilliant mind and beautiful spirit are indeed reflected brightly in this book. In 1996, she became one of the Saints in Glory.

To the authors and publishers of quotations in the book for permission to include their copyrighted messages. These are acknowledged in another section.

To E. Stanley Jones, my spiritual mentor, for giving me a clearer concept of The Way. The dedication section will tell the story of a flaming evangelist to the world.

To all friends and prayer partners whose faithful intercession is surely part of the divine guidance and grace needed for the writing of this book. Many of these friends are in nursing homes and in non-retirement centers, ministers indeed to me.

To Dr. Theodore E. Conrad, college and seminary professor, scholar and theologian and friend, who at age 97 carries on fruitful ministries from his wheelchair, blessing me in our many visits and in several Bible study groups. I write about him in this book.

To Ross Foley, Pastor of Faith Covenant Church in Burnsville, Minnesota, for permission to quote from his sermon. Each month he sends me copies of his powerful sermons that challenge and bless me.

To John Jurkow for his discerning message in the book and for the memory of his weekly visits that blessed me richly. John died very suddenly in March of 2002.

To the publisher of this book, Lutheran Colportage Service of Minneapolis, Minnesota. For 70 years, this center has been publishing the good news of the divine love across the city, nation and world. And more—across inner-city streets in personal evangelism and social ministries. I am happy to have the Lutheran Colportage Service symbol of the flame and cross on this book.

To Perry Duff Smith, Jr., a specialist in the field of graphic design who captures the message of the book in his special art cover. He is also the layout artist. His professional guidance in the long journey toward publication has given me confidence and assurance.

To Carol Smith for her typing of many versions of the book, for her processing of dozens of tapes and for her editing skills. She has shown patience and poise under the pressure of deadlines and has spent innumerable hours as a research specialist in securing copyright privileges.

Above all, praise is due to my Lord and Saviour for permitting me to write this book at age 92. His promise in Psalm 32:8 has sustained me:

"I will instruct you and teach you the way you should go;
I will counsel you with my eye upon you."

Acknowledgments ♩

Used with the permission of Simon & Schuster, Inc. Taken from *The Cost of Discipleship* by Dietrich Bonhoffer, translated from the German by R. H. Fuller with some revisions by Irmgard Booth. Copyright © 1959 by SCM Press, Ltd. (page xii).

Taken from *From Grey to Gold* by Marta Berg. Copyright © 1995 by Marta Berg. BCB Books. Used by permission (pages 11, 32, 63, 81).

Taken from "Awareness" by Miriam Teichner (page 17).

Taken from *God So Loved* by Walter Barlow. Copyright © MCM-LII. Used by permission of Baker Book Company, Grand Rapids, MI (page 28).

Taken from *The Applause of Heaven* by Max Lucado. Copyright © 1990. W Publishing Group, Nashville, Tennessee. All rights reserved (page 30).

Taken from *My Utmost for His Highest* by Oswald Chambers. Copyright © 1935 by Dodd Mead & Co., renewed © 1963 by the Oswald Chambers Publications Assn. Ltd. and is used by permission of Discovery House Publishers, Box 3566, Grand Rapids, MI 49501. All rights reserved (pages 31, 37, 40, 52).

Taken from *In Christ* by E. Stanley Jones. Copyright © 1961 by Abingdon Press. Used by permission of Abingdon Press (pages 38, 42).

Taken from *Seen and Unseen* by Marta Berg. Copyright © 1991 by Marta Berg. Winston-Derek Publishers, Inc. (pages 45, 50, 73, 98, 113).

Taken from *Oh How He Loves You* by Corrie ten Boom. Copyright © 1977. Used by permission of Baker Book Company, Grand Rapids, MI. (page 61)

Taken from *The Great House of God* by Max Lucado. Copyright © 1997. W Publishing Group, Nashville, Tennessee. All rights reserved (pages 67, 77).

IN PUBLIC DOMAIN

*I pay tribute to the unknown
authors for stories and
illustrations which could not be
traced to the proper source.
I apologize for any such instances.
If you recognize an uncited story,
please let me know and the
publisher and I will be sure to
acknowledge the author
in future printings.*